Fiction Writing Maps

A Step-By-Step Guide To Characters

JACKIE ST. JAMES

Jackie St. James/Five Smooth Stones Publishing

2433 S. University Dr.

Fort Worth, Texas 76109

www.fictionwritingmaps.com

Publisher's Note: Names, characters, places, and incidents are a product of the author's imagination. Locales and public names are sometimes used for atmospheric purposes. Any resemblance to actual people, living or dead, or to businesses, companies, events, institutions, or locales is completely coincidental.

Ordering Information:

Quantity sales. Special discounts are available on quantity purchases by corporations, associations, and others. For details, contact the "Special Sales Department" at the address above.

Fiction Writing Maps: A Step-By-Step Guide To Characters/Jackie St. James. – 1st ed.

ISBN 978-0-9964153-6-1

eBook ISBN 978-0-9964153-5-4

For Clint, who has more brilliant ideas in one afternoon than there are grains of sand on a beach.

"Everyone has one good story in them.

Getting it out of them is the hard part."

Jackie St. James

TABLE OF CONTENTS

INTRODUCTION 9

    About The Maps 10

    Defining The Problem 11

    Parts Unknown 12

    How This Book Works 13

    What The Maps Are Not 14

    Why The Work Is Worth It 16

    A Word On Mentor Texts 17

    Get In Touch @ Keep In Touch 19

CHAPTER ONE 20

THE FIRST DRAFT 20

CHAPTER TWO 23

THE CHARACTER INTRODUCTION 23

    The Short List 24

    Character Sketch 25

    Character Body Type 27

    Gender & Age Range 30

    Hair & Facial Features 32

    Emotional State & Temperament 37

CHAPTER THREE 42

CONVEYING CHARACTER 42

    Getting To Know Your Character 43

Quick Write First 44

Character Corroboration 44

Describing Emotion 46

Scaffolding Off Physical Traits 52

CHAPTER FOUR **57**

MOTIVATING & ACTIVATING THE CHARACTER 57

Activating Character 58

Maslow's Hierarchy 62

The Greatest Is Love 63

Fear Works, Too 64

CHAPTER FIVE **68**

A NEW SPIN ON ARCHETYPES 68

Spinning Your Archetype 69

Mix It Up 70

Stretch The Boundaries 71

Hero or Villain? 72

CHAPTER SIX **77**

CREATING HISTORY & PARSING BACKSTORY 77

Building Backstory 79

One Piece At A Time 80

Anecdotes 81

Time Travel 81

Classic Anecdote 82

Musings of Characters 84

Quick Transitions 91

CHAPTER SEVEN 94

MASTERING THE VIGNETTE.. 94

    Searching For A Solution 95

    Thinking Inside The Box 96

    How Authors Use The Vignette 99

    Building A Vignette 101

    Bits & Pieces 103

    Planning The Vignette 105

    Mastering The Vignette 106

CHAPTER EIGHT 107

SYMBOLISM & CHARACTERIZATION 107

    Symbols In Literature 108

    Finding A Character's Symbol 109

    Historical References 110

    Symbolism In Literature 111

    What Does My Character Resemble? 114

    Callie's Outward Characteristics 115

    Quick Write 115

    Examples In Fiction 119

    Final Thoughts On Symbols 122

CHAPTER NINE 125

HEROIC TRAITS 125

    The Five Key Traits of Heroes.. 126

    The Ordinary Extraordinary 126

    Command Respect From Peers 127

    Convert "Difficult" To "Simple" 129

Frail Human Nature 130

Willpower 132

Finding The Perfect Flaw 134

CHAPTER TEN **140**

THE WRITING COMPASS 140

    Crafting The Scene 141

    The Basic Scene Template 143

    Character Template Example I 144

    Decoding The Mentor Text 145

    Applying The Template 146

    Discussion 150

    Character Template Example II 151

    Exploring An Opening Template 152

    Opening Template 153

    Template For Two Characters 155

    Discussion 158

    Conclusion 159

    Filmography 161

    Resources 163

        Character Archetypes 163

        Writer's Resources 170

        Suggested Reading 171

INDEX **173**

INTRODUCTION

> *Most people sit down to write a novel without ever having done it before.*
>
> *Is it any wonder that so few people actually finish a novel?*

Fiction writing boils down to understanding how to plug your unique ideas into the framework of a novel. Like any other major endeavor, a novel has a unique design and an explicit process for using that design. Though the design is simple, understanding the process is more challenging. The process requires a writer to take the story playing in their head, translate it into plot, characters, scenes and setting, and transfer all of those lovely words into the novel framework.

The ideas are always the easiest part. It's the words and novel framework that create a huge stumbling block for most writers. Good writers understand this. The writers who go on to publish well-received novels do one thing differently than everyone else—they study how to write a novel—and master it.

The good news is that you can, too.

Up until now, there was no 'how to' for novel writing that outlines a clear path. Fortunately, the new era in publication has given rise to information, tools and resources that have made writing more accessible. My hope is that The Fiction Writing Maps will clarify and simplify the novel writing process so that all writers have a greater chance of success.

About The Maps

In 2013, I restructured my professional life to take advantage of my graduate degree in English. I designed an online platform to assist graduate students who needed research and organization for dissertations and other scholarly papers. From there, I branched out to add editors for Google AdWords campaigns, website content, blogs and book reviews.

We had weekly, often daily, requests for editing and proofreading of half-finished manuscripts. Many of these stories were brilliant ideas with well-developed plot lines, but they were all incomplete. The writers had begun their novel, but stalled out when they came to places in the writing process where they couldn't transfer their vision into the novel design. Unwilling to admit defeat, these brave souls looked for help.

Over time, we found that the issues our clients struggled with were almost universal. In fact, we were answering so many of the same questions that we began compiling a list of writing FAQs to address these issues. One chilly afternoon in 2015, I sat down to finalize answers to those questions.

Hot chocolate at hand, I read through some manuscript submissions and focused on the common stumbling blocks these writers encountered. Common themes began to emerge. With each manuscript I read and each question I answered, I became more determined to map a path through these areas of uncertainty and chaos for my clients. Finally, the problem distilled down to three large pieces of the writing puzzle. Characters, Setting and Scene. These areas are so broad that I had to distill them down, target the precise location where writers had gone off track and identify what happened.

After weeks combing Amazon, Barnes & Nobel the library for resources, I realized with shock there were no resources for immediate, helpful fixes to these common writing problems. I found books about "how to hone your writing," "find character motivation" and "build fictional worlds." But I found no resource that guided the writer through the novel design. There was a big, black hole in the literature that no one had even tried to fill.

I pinpointed the problem, but the solution looked dreadfully complicated - as in $x^{infinity}$ complicated. How do you explain the creative process of writing a novel? How do you show each writer how to plug their own ideas into that framework?

Defining The Problem

I thought that if I focused on the places where clients stumbled, I might be able to redirect those missteps and offer viable solutions for fixing them or even avoiding them. I began the project as a bolder and more comprehensive version that spanned Character, Scene and Setting in one volume. I soon found that I needed to focus on character first, but I kept in mind that the overlapping threads of Character, Scene and Setting would all come together by the end of the third book.

Character came first because from a structural standpoint, the description of characters and explanations of their personalities, motives and connections usually occurs before anything else in the novel. It seemed sensible to start from there. After all, it is your characters who shoulder the burden of the telling. They speak to one another, about one another and drive the narrative forward. Without a clear vision of who your players are, no story can truly begin.

Characters can be simple or elaborate, but they all demand the same complement, the same package of information. They're fictional people plotted into a piece of writing in that follows a predictable design. When I had singled out characters as the launching pad for the first set of Maps, I began to tackle the most frequent questions:

- How do I introduce a new Character?
- How do I choose which character details are important?
- How can I give information on characters without sounding like a boring info dump?
- My main character just isn't interesting...how do I fix that?

With each new thread of answer, a writing web began to emerge. Many months passed before I stumbled over the common thread that united them all. And it was relatively simple. With a design in mind, I set out to fill the black hole in writing resources with a set of maps that guided writers through character creation, setting design and integration into solid, substantive scenes.

Parts Unknown

The goal was clear. Now I had to distill a lifetime of reading novels and writing pedagogy down to a universal, easy-to-follow framework. I had to *show* fiction writers how to design great characters in a step-by-step process. Like a literary version of orienteering, I pored through novels to discover precisely what I needed to define. Then I began planning and laying out The Maps.

The more I pored over the writing of other authors, the clearer the design for The Maps became. It took countless hours, a plethora of legal pads, Scrivener editing and a good deal of Avoca Misty Valley coffee to draft *The Fiction Writing Maps*. I include in this work the links to the resources that supported my research. I've added that list in the Resources section so that writers who want to dig deeper can see the path I took to arrive at the final product for *The Fiction Writing Maps.*

How This Book Works

A Step-By-Step Guide To Characters is a process-driven approach to novel writing that will:

- Help you understand how character functions in the novel—both in the 'micro' spaces of writing and the larger scope of the plot

- Show you how to describe characters in evocative language that translates to visual images

- Help you decide what to include when introducing each character

- Scaffold your writing to deepen character development quickly and easily

- Apply this mapping process to your novel in progress

- Dispel the misconception that only "true" authors can achieve industry results

Each chapter of the book deals with one aspect of building a fictional character. I provide examples from Classic Fiction as well as examples created specifically for this book in order to illustrate how each writing technique works. At the end of the chapter, I break the technique down in steps to help you turn "concept" into "writing." The Concept, Examples and Guide system creates a character-building design that ends with your own substantive, unique writing. The Maps takes writing a step further. You'll flex your character writing skills and generate the muscle memory that allows you to dash off interesting characters quickly rather than agonizing over character development.

What The Maps Are Not

Maps, by design, act as a chart to get travelers from starting point to final destination in their journey by the best route with as few useless detours as possible. There are those who believe that writing a novel just requires you to produce as many words as possible every day and then choose from those 300,000 words. I've seen this in action and can verify that this is not only the most ineffective and most grueling process, but also the least successful method of novel writing. This process does not build your understanding of novel design, it does not make you a more adept writer and it virtually ensures that you will make the same mistakes with book two....if there is ever even a book one.

Jamming out thousands of words a day in the hope of coming up with something brilliant is like shooting skeet into an empty sky and counting on birds to fly past. Volume doesn't guarantee substance or cohesion. It guarantees inches of ink and paper.

Good writing is built on goals; the goal is to produce a well-written manuscript. That require planning and work. I can hear every pantser howling 'No!' to that statement. But let's be realistic: baking a cake, planting a garden or building a website takes planning and work. I'm sure that we can agree that designing, building and writing a fictional world populated with dynamic characters is a great deal more difficult than anything on that previous list.

So, I offer my "go to" visual exercise that illustrates this point:

Picture yourself standing in the center of an 8 x 8 room with four walls. On one wall is a dartboard. Your objective is to hit that board with any one of the three darts you hold in your hand.

The goal is to hit a bull's-eye, but anything close will do. While you know the dartboard is located at eye level, you can't see anything past the inky blackness that surrounds you.

At the signal, you take the first of the darts, aim roughly at eye level and throw. You hear the hollow 'thunk' of a complete miss.

You turn a quarter turn, thinking perhaps you'll have a better shot at another wall. You aim again, throw and hear the sound of failure. Again.

Now you have a single dart—a single chance—left. Suddenly, one event occurs that changes the entire dynamic. This one event exponentially increases your odds of hitting the target and perhaps even landing a bull's-eye.

Someone turns on the light.

The Fiction Writing Maps is that light. Throughout the book, I provide examples from well-respected authors, explain each approach to writing characters, and show you how to apply each technique to your own writing to create your own deep, dynamic characters. The Maps take you from plodding and uncertain writing to the superhighway of fictional character design. Working with The Maps will make writing faster, more professional and more enjoyable for you—and for your readers.

The Fiction Writing Maps will transform your novel writing. No more hollow failures, no more lost chances, no more stumbling in the dark. You can always be a pantser tomorrow if you still want to go that route. Why not save time and try The Maps just once?

Why The Work Is Worth It

If you want to create characters who are robust and lifelike enough to carry the weight of the story, you have to design and write multilayered individuals who feel authentic. I simplified the elements that good writers use to construct these true-to-life characters. No, we won't be focusing on character dossiers and character bio sheets from the internet (though some of those can be helpful for keeping track of details). Instead, we'll examine how great writers use character design and duplicate that process in actual writing.

In each section, I'll explain one aspect of character, give examples, then scaffold off those examples to examine them at work in a practical writing technique. Each section will build on what you've learned in the previous section. This will not only help deepen the character that you've created, but it will also build your writing skill as you progress.

The most important benefit of these exercises is that you build a better understanding of the writing process and produce clear, professional and "immediately operational" prose that fulfills a specific purpose in your novel. While we won't write the entire novel together character by character, you will see the individual techniques for good character development at work throughout the book.

If you know what you need help with, you may jump ahead to that section of the book. No doubt, you'll tweak The Maps to fit your own style and needs. If you're like me, you prefer to cut to the chase. To facilitate that, I've added some "Cut To The Chase" boxes that encapsulate the most relevant parts in each section. Look for them as you read and refer to them as you continue through the book.

A Word On Mentor Texts

The examples are by far the most important part in each of the chapters. Through Mentor Texts, I'll show you how the best authors generated characters with simple and exquisite prose. Each of the examples is broken down with explanations that peel back the layers of writing and explain the meaning behind it.

I share examples from author texts easily located for free from Project Gutenberg. https://www.gutenberg.org. Since some of the older literature isn't to the taste of more modern readers, I've augmented those texts with additional examples.

These examples are unique to this piece of literature and based on entirely fictitious characters. Drafting these examples was part of the fun of writing this resource. I plotted a quick story and created characters just as you will do. These pieces are captioned with *FWM* and have the name of the character listed. I created these excerpts without agonizing over them too much because they're meant to exemplify 'Quick Writes' before editing. Other excerpts were pulled from the works of Clint Wilson. These excerpts are listed by title of the work and author.

Cast of Characters

Calendar "Callie" McCrae	Carter Wilkins
Talvert Carmichael	Sio Goodman
Charles Goodman	Thomaz Lenz
Ian Hagler	Judge Hagler
Padre Piu	Catherine Coullder

Get In Touch @ Keep In Touch

I wrote *The Fiction Writing Maps* with the sole purpose of supporting writers. I want your writing venture to end in success and not to fall by the wayside as "the best book never written." I believe that building a writing community with a free flow of ideas helps each of us attain more than we could have achieved alone.

I've provided this guide for writers who want to make an investment in their skill, but don't have the resources of time or money to take an online writing course or get a degree in creative writing. I'd love to know what worked, what didn't work and which writing tools you found useful.

Let me know your thoughts and ideas for subsequent updates and books in the series. Shoot me a line if you want to add your own writing passage to the next *Fiction Writing Maps* and receive full credit within the book.

You can always contact me at admin@fictionwritingmaps.com stop by www.fictionwritingmaps.com or join the discussion #FictionWritingMaps.

CHAPTER ONE
The First Draft

Before you dive into The Maps, pull out a piece of writing in which you introduce a character (if you have one) or create a piece for an entirely new character. It doesn't need to be more than a paragraph long—no pressure. The goal here isn't to create a perfect piece of writing—far from it. I want you to write quickly & intuitively, accept all of the imperfections. Leave big blanks if your pen hovers for more than a second. Just focus on creating a character introduction in whatever form you want.

I'll wait ☺

This piece of writing represents your writing in all of its uniqueness and imperfection. This is you at the threshold of your ability. Maybe you're excited by what you've written or maybe you're frustrated. If you're excited, "Yea!" If you're frustrated, you're in good company. Great company, in fact. C. S Lewis and Tolkien are just two of your peer group who spring to mind. Lewis and Tolkien developed a profound friendship that blossomed into a large and exuberant writing group. In those meetings once or twice a week, Tolkien might read the next chapter in his series and get critiques and feedback.

Getting feedback on the work product is what you're doing now. Rather than having a writing group of Oxford scholars, you're going to use the *work* of those scholars to evaluate your own writing. This is a quick, data-oriented exercise to help you break down what you've put in your introduction. Read through your sentences one by one to evaluate *what information* you've given the reader.

I've put an example below from *Emma* to illustrate the process:

Classic Fiction

"Harriet Smith was the natural daughter of somebody. Somebody had placed her, several years back, at Mrs. Goddard's school, and somebody had lately raised her from the condition of scholar to that of parlour–boarder. This was all that was generally known of her history. She had no visible friends but what had been acquired at Highbury, and was now just returned from a long visit in the country to some young ladies who had been at school there with her.

She was a very pretty girl, and her beauty happened to be of a sort which Emma particularly admired. She was short, plump, and fair, with a fine bloom, blue eyes, light hair, regular features, and a look of great sweetness, and, before the end of the evening, Emma was as much pleased with her manners as her person, and quite determined to continue the acquaintance."

Jane Austen. *Emma*

Background: Harriet's birth, her schooling, her friendship and her recent travel.

Physical description: General outward description as "pretty"

Body Type: "short, plump"

Hair: "light hair"

Eyes: "blue eyes"

Facial Features: " ...a fine bloom.." "regular features"

Temperament: "pleased with her manners..."

Type: "of a sort which Emma particularly liked..."

Read through your own writing and see if you can break down data points like these that appear in your writing. How closely do your data points match Austen's? As you do this, it might strike you that Austen's description of Harriet is relatively simple compared to yours. It might even occur to you that you've wasted a great deal of time trying to describe a character's eyes when Austen—in her infinite wisdom—used only one adjective for Harriet's. This brings us to the beginning of *A Step-By-Step Guide To Characters*. Here we start to answer the questions so many other have asked, beginning with "what do I need to introduce a character?" Keep your work handy because you'll revise it as we move along.

CHAPTER TWO

The Character Introduction

> At the end of this exercise, you should have a basic description of your character that includes height, body type, age, gender, hair, facial features and emotional state. This should be ready to import directly into your novel.

Every story begins with Character, and the first few pages of a novel are prime literary real estate. Here you have a fleeting opportunity to grab and keep your readers' attention by introducing a relatable, interesting character.

But how do you do that? What details do you highlight right away? And how do describe a character for the first time without sounding like a dating site? These questions—and others along the same lines—plague writers as they draft that first introduction to character.

Though you might see your character vividly in your mind's eye, writing what you see can be difficult. In fact, the affliction commonly referred to as 'Writer's

Block' is often nothing more than the pressure of choosing the right words to convey that visual image. The good news is that there's an easy way around that block—a way to leapfrog over wasted time and drop right into the substance of your character.

You've read countless novels in many genres and you can pinpoint the exact places where an author brings a new character into the story. If you went back to read and compare some of those passages, you'd see that even though they're different, they have significant things in common. Understand that *your* character introductions, though different, should have those same components. How many times have you broken those introductions down, pinpointed those components of a good character introduction and then applied them to your writing?

No judgement here. However, if the answer is somewhere between zero and three, then you should read this chapter. In it, I cover exactly what's needed to create a character introduction. At the end of this chapter, you'll write the same quick introduction for your character, using the exact elements from the example to build a character of your own.

The Short List

In each of the classics and best sellers that I researched for this book, I found enormous variety in the ways writers present characters for the first time. But there were some things they all had in common. Those things fall under the heading of "The Short List" These are incredibly basic, self-evident points of description that you need to present for every major character and most minor characters. Since this is also the first exercise, we're going to keep the examples short, simple and straightforward. We'll also stick with basic narration in these examples to keep the focus tight.

To begin, here's the short list of details that other authors include in the basic character introduction:

- Body Type
- Gender/Age Range
- Hair & Facial Features
- Clothing & Physical Features
- Emotional State

This brief list spans literature from *Pride and Prejudice* to *The Adventures of Sherlock Holmes* and everything in between. It outlines a standard method that worked as well for Sir Arthur Conan Doyle as it did for C. S. Lewis. Readers must be able to "see" your character, form a visual image of a person before they can engage in the story.

To get you started, I've given classic examples in fiction as well as those I created for this book. Each example gives a breakdown by character trait and discusses the most significant points of that example. I've isolated simple, effective writing to show you how to plan and draft your own character introductions quickly and easily.

Character Sketch

Much as an artist creates an outer boundary for a portrait to show the shape and form of the subject, you'll create the same boundaries with words. When readers open your book, they hold examples in their mind of every person they have seen and every character they have read. It is your job to use a character introduction to winnow down the millions of possible visual images your readers have that describe "a person" down to just one person: *your character.*

Description of height and body type help readers visualize the outline of your character, much as a pencil sketch would do. This is important because it is often the first bit of information that your reader has to help bring the character into focus. Size and stature of a character gives the reader a wealth of information beyond the obvious. These two physical traits act as gateways to explore everything from a character's vulnerability, to their health or their ability to take on the physical challenges that might occur in the plot.

Issues of size can also give us insight into the emotional make-up of a character. Just like the rest of us, characters can have their own hang-ups about body image and size. A character might be a committed runner or a girl who's felt too tall all her life. Whichever path you take, it's intriguing to play with combinations, explore this area to look for character hang-ups, strengths and weaknesses. The important point to remember is that these outward descriptions go deeper than surface level. If you're focusing on the detail of height, make it count. Use it to explore old wounds from middle school or make it relevant to the present moment. If you can't do that, then deal with it quickly and move on to the next detail.

Character Body Type

> *Body type is the first and most basic bit of information that the reader needs in order to "see" your character.*

If you wonder why your character's body type is even relevant to the story, I recommend you watch the beginning of *Gone With the Wind*. The character of Scarlett O'Hara leaps to life in the novel using little more than a corset and a rebellious attitude. Mitchell even mentions the exact size of Scarlett's waist when introducing the character because it was relevant measuring stick in society at the time. When Scarlett refuses to eat breakfast and prances onto the front porch to find a husband, the reader discovers deeper social issues and dynamics of relationships, but the vehicle for introducing everything was Scarlett's body type and the size of her waist.

Sir Arthur Conan Doyle was the master of introducing characters using only the basics. He also used body type time and time again as a means of introducing characters. Doyle dealt in mysteries and gave careful thought to limiting the information he revealed and making it count. The backwards design of this writing results in well-crafted character sketches that are easy to study. As you read these, you might see how quickly you can design a character using very limited information.

In each of these first examples, I've shown you the same quick path to character creation using straightforward and simple narratives.

Classic Fiction

> *"A man entered who could hardly have been less than six feet six inches in height, with the chest and limbs of a Hercules."*
>
> Arthur Conan Doyle. *The Adventures of Sherlock Holmes*

- *Height:* Writers rarely—if ever—have a measuring tape handy in the novel so height is often provided by general size or through comparison to other characters.

- *Hint:* Look for a marker within your setting that might help describe the height or body type of your character.

- *Body Type:* Doyle uses an allusion to Hercules to describe this character. He doesn't waste time detailing his physique because the mythological hero is known to virtually all readers and elicits an immediate physical comparison.

- *Why It Works:* It took only one sentence to paint a general, but vivid, description of the character The reference to Hercules adds a possibility of menace to the moment that creates an immediate air of tension.

- *Possibilities:* Plot point. From here, a writer could move in any direction—from imminent physical danger to a build-up of plot in which this Hercules character features as a suspect. This all occurs within the space of 24 short words.

FWM: Calendar McCrae

> *"The girl sitting in his office chair was barely taller than a teenager, with the slender build and the pixie-faced, pointed chin of Tinker Belle."*
>
> *Fiction Writing Maps: A Step-By-Step Guide To Characters*

- *Height:* I stayed relatively close to Doyle's example to show you how effectively it works in modern fiction. I imported my character description of body type and added some other features to change the visual image.

- *Body Type:* In keeping with the body type that Doyle described, I provided a comparison that is well-known to most readers.

- *Hint:* Make your descriptors meaningful. I used Tinker Belle here and I will mention it at least two more times in the novel. To mention it once and then leave it is pointless. Readers hate that. Make a descriptor count or don't use it at all.

- *Why It Works:* This is a simple way to present characters when you want to move quickly into the story.

Gender & Age Range

> *Gender and age range can be quick, succinct pieces of information that you add before moving on with character introduction. You can introduce them explicitly or implicitly, but don't try to skip them.*

Gender and age range are two of the most obvious and significant points to deal with in creating your character. As with body type and height, these basic details are imperative. While there are occasions when gender and age become important to the narrative, more often than not you simply want to present them and get them out of the way. Below are some examples of quick management of gender and age. Later, we will delve deeper into scaffolding techniques for these two elements.

Classic Fiction

> *"He's a young man, Mr. Merryweather, but he is at the head of his profession, and I would rather have my bracelets on him than on any criminal in London. He's a remarkable man, is young John Clay. His grandfather was a royal duke, and he himself has been to Eton and Oxford."*
>
> **Arthur Conan Doyle.** *The Adventures of Sherlock Holmes*

- *Gender/Age:* For most characters, age and gender need to be addressed at some point. However, unless they are significant in some way, they fall under a very general heading. In many cases, they are dealt with succinctly and with a minimum of fuss.

- *Why It Works:* In the one sentence, "He's a remarkable man, is young John Clay," both items are presented and the syntax—though more antiquated—is basic, flawless and does its job perfectly.

FWM: Calendar McCrae

> "She was only five years out of college, but had already made a name for herself as the most capable and trustworthy private investigator in Texas. Randall Mills, her closest competition, had two decades of experience on her, but a steadily building drinking habit had also given him a reputation as being loose-lipped when the liquor flowed. People who required confidentiality went to Calendar."
>
> *Fiction Writing Maps: A Step-By-Step Guide To Characters*

- *Gender/Age:* I didn't state the character's age explicitly, but used college as a guidepost for age.
- *Why It Works:* Not only does the reader get the important information about the character's age and gender, but also information about where Cal fits into the social order of the novel as it begins.
- *Possibilities:* From here, I could focus on Cal's reputation since it was a key point in the paragraph or I could shift to the people who hired her and take off on a plot line. All that matters is that the character information transitions smoothly forward.

Hair & Facial Features

> *Hair and facial features are the primary source that writers use to begin distinguishing their characters from the outside in. This explanation will be quick and succinct with minor characters. With your major characters, these are gateways to deeper characterization.*

Like it or not, when we meet someone for the first time, the unconscious questions that we ask ourselves are "How is this person like me?" and "What's different about this person?" Those two assessments are rapidly programmed into that first encounter—often without us ever having realized that we've done it. Readers ask the very same questions when meeting your character for the first time. It's up to you to use these two features to build that first rung of characterization.

This process of assessing is ingrained, instinctive human behavior. It's how we learn to tell one another apart and examine how we *feel* about one another. While body type is usually one of the first distinctions that we notice on the outside, we begin to make out who a person is on the *inside* from the expressions that flit across their face as we interact with them.

As they would in a real scenario, readers form impressions of a character through the description of hair and facial features. Many aspects of a character can be determined from the face and hair, but readers make three assessments right away from a character's hair, face and facial expression: physical appeal, trustworthiness and competence.

Classic Fiction

> *"Her fair hair was very fair, her lovely grey eyes were very lovely and grey, her dark eyelashes were very dark, her white skin was very white, her red mouth was very red. She was extravagantly slender— the merest thread of a girl, though not without little curves beneath her thin frock where little curves should be."*
>
> Elizabeth Von Arnim. *The Enchanted April*

- *Hair & Face:* The description of hair and face focuses on the contrast of colors first, and then on the stark contrasts that the viewer sees.

- *Body Type:* The body description reinforces the ideal of a perfectly formed and delicate female.

- *Why It Works:* The repetition of "very, very" works in this passage because Von Arnim illustrates girlhood at the extreme. In this character, she depicts the superlative, aided by the repetition of adjectives.

- *Possibilities:* As you might imagine, a beginning like this is not common when introducing character. However, it does push the boundaries in an interesting way that begs attention.

Classic Fiction

> *"From the lower part of the face he appeared to be a man of strong character, with a thick, hanging lip, and a long, straight chin, suggestive of resolution pushed to the length of obstinacy."*
>
> Arthur Conan Doyle. *The Adventures of Sherlock Holmes*

- *Face:* The description of face is often used to reveal character traits such as Doyle does here.

- *Character Traits:* Doyle uses specific facial features as evidence of the character's obstinacy.

- *Why It Works:* Rather than having facial features stand alone, make them count by linking them to specific character traits. This kind of visual evidence is powerful. We make daily determinations about complete strangers based on nothing more than the set of their jaw and a passing look on their face.

- *Possibilities:* From here, you might focus on dialogue or some interaction that reinforces the character trait of obstinacy. Remember that these traits don't travel alone. Anger is the close companion of obstinacy. This might be a place to work towards a plot point that integrates story narrative with this character trait.

FWM: Calendar McCrae

"*Her face radiated sharp intelligence and interest. Her eyes never stopped in their course, sweeping the room, studying everything from the papers strewn over every inch of Judge Haglar's desk, to the picture of his wife, to the empty glass on the console behind the desk. There was, in those eyes, a knife-edged scrutiny and youthfulness that were entirely at odds with one another.*"

Fiction Writing Maps: A Step-By-Step Guide To Characters

- *Face:* I used Doyle's example only as a starting point, then allowed the eyes to reveal the character.

- *Eyes:* I wanted to show the careful, analytical side of Cal's personality at work.

- *Why It Works:* Arguably, it doesn't work as well as Doyle's example. It would benefit from revision, but it does the job of getting the information across.

- *Possibilities:* From here, I will probably move to an action in the scene. However, I won't leave the scene without shifting back once more to her eyes. This is another key feature of creating what I call 'sticky character traits.' You make them stick in iterations that keep their meaning relevant. If you're going to say it once and never revisit it, ask yourself if it's truly important.

Classic Fiction

> *"Miss Honeychurch, disjoined from her music stool, was a young lady with a quantity of dark hair and a very pretty, pale, undeveloped face."*
>
> E. M. Forster. *A Room With A View*

- *Face:* Forster describes Lucy's features as "a pretty, pale, undeveloped face" in this excerpt. This isn't because he can't or won't describe Lucy Honeychurch. It's because the word "undeveloped" is the best descriptor of *who* Lucy is at the beginning of the novel. The story traces Lucy's journey from relative innocence to independence. So, while the word "undeveloped" might seem like a generality, it does lead the reader closer to a visual picture of Lucy. Forster uses this outward physical detail to help his Readers understand that Lucy's personality stands on the threshold of change.

- *Hair:* "A quantity of dark hair" is all we get from Forster here. Again, it seems like he's peppering the description with banalities. However, Lucy is presented as the physical idealization of the Edwardian young woman. A fun fact to note for the literature geeks is that *hair*–in this case, an abundance of it–is a common sexual symbol in literature. In other words, Lucy has an unmeasured capacity for desire.

- *Why It Works:* Though you will likely want to write more straightforward passages for the modern reader, it's useful to see how you also might manipulate the social and sexual climate of your novel to add an immediate undercurrent of meaning in one small description.

- *Possibilities:* This quick description begs for action, dialogue and then more detailed description afterwards.

FWM: Calendar McCrae

"Calendar McCrae, perched in the chair across from Talvert, was in her mid-twenties. She had the pale, slightly freckled skin that comes with Irish blood. If left down, her strawberry blonde hair would have hung in loose waves to the middle of her back. This morning, she'd coiled it into a tight knot, jammed a pencil through it instantly forgotten about it. Now she reached up and grabbed the pencil, paying no attention to Talvert's reaction as the curls broke free."

Fiction Writing Maps: A Step-By-Step Guide To Characters

- *Face:* I deviated from Forster's example to create a voice of my own here, but it was helpful to have that example nevertheless.

- *Hair:* In keeping with the spirit of the Forster example, I've added the description of hair. I might have left it out, but that it will feature as a tag for Calendar throughout the novel.

- *Why It Works:* Though it doesn't mirror the Forster passage exactly, you can see how the mentor text helped to formulate a quick character description with very little.

- *Possibilities:* From here, I'll move to either the setting, an opening dialogue, or I might make a quick visual introduction of the character sitting across from Calendar. I won't leave this passage without mentioning Cal's hair or the pencil again since I've positioned both of them in the scene.

Emotional State & Temperament

Emotion—more than any other single element—is the bait that hooks the reader. A great writer, like an expert fisherman, chooses the bait to suit the fish. Spend some time thinking about what matters most to your readers as you open on a character introduction. What's the bait that tempts them? What will lure them above all else? These are the emotions you want to leverage.

You want the character on the page to evoke a response from your reader. In order to evoke a response, you need reader buy-in. Your character must first convince the reader that he's real, and then do or say something that extracts an emotional response. How does a writer do this?

Let's look at the character Harry Potter in the first book, *The Sorcerer's Stone*. The story opens on a young boy living in a cupboard under the stairs, oppressed and bullied by people dumber than dirt. This story premise is one that every adolescent, worldwide, can appreciate. Rowling's story opener generates an immediate and universal emotional tug by using a conflict that is familiar to every one of her readers. Who hasn't felt oppressed at one time or another? Who hasn't wished that some fairy godmother-like figure would come and rescue them from that oppression?

As you draft the emotional appeal of your character introduction, ask yourself what your readers have in common. What have they all gone through at one time or another? Have they felt isolated? Misunderstood? Worried that they'll fail in some miserable, public way? Spend some time digging through the psychology of your group if only for a few hours. You might latch onto a gem of an idea to help generate an opening as brilliant as J. K. Rowling. Once you have that, you're ready to write.

The art of creating character lies in weaving the details of character back and forth between the outward appearance, the inner life of the character and the events as they're happening in the present moment of the story. When introducing a character, you need to transition back and forth in a way that mimics reality. Our eyes sweep back and forth between the person we're meeting, the people around us, our immediate environment and then back to the person we are meeting. I'm building on the previous example, adding the character's emotional state and including that sweeping motion so that you can see it in context.

Have a look at this quickly sketched example:

"I saw him go that way. Better hurry, little lady, if you want to catch him." Calendar looked over her shoulder to find who had spoken to her. A large man pointed vaguely in the direction of the town square. His smile, more leering than helpful, showed two rows of yellowed teeth. Calendar noticed a trail of something that looked like gravy down the front of his faded plaid shirt that was pulled so tight that two buttons remained open at the bottom to allow his belly to spill out over the front of his pants. Her stomach heaved in disgust, but she muttered a thank you and shot off in the direction he had indicated."

The Fiction Writing Maps: A Step-By-Step Guide To Characters

And that's it.

It took less than five minutes to write this character opening. The short piece has two, roughly sketched characters on the page and offers a crumb of emotional charge in a short space at the end. The opening included a brief observation by the other character. Then, the exchange ended in an action by the observing character. This quick 'back-and-forth' between characters is often all that writers begin with when introducing a character. Once you've mastered it, you'll see how simple it becomes to go one step deeper with every subsequent interaction, offering more and more insight into the characters by parsing out detail as you progress. That's all you need to get started.

Character Introduction

Step 1: What is your character's body type and gender? Why is your character's body type relevant to characterization or within the larger context of the novel? Can you use it as a gateway to describe your character's lifestyle, profession, relationships and self-image? Write those out now in complete, unedited thoughts

_____

_____

_____

_____

_____

Step 2: What is your character's size? Find a point of comparison within the novel or through other characters to show your character's size. Is your character's size relevant in any other way? Write those out now in complete, unedited thoughts

_____

_____

_____

_____

Step 3: What is your character's age range? What facial features detail your character's age? Can you connect the two with relevant exposition, an anecdote or through the point of view of another character in the opening scene? Write those out now in complete, unedited thoughts.

_____

_____

_____

_____

_____

Step 4: What emotion will you use to lure your reader? What tempts most readers of this genre? What tempts readers in this age group and demographic? Will you focus on a fear or a victory charge? With what bait can you make your readers go 'all in' for your character? Can you define her temperament to clarify her inner landscape? Choose one word, connect it to a thought and a character emotion. Write that out now in complete, unedited thoughts.

_____

_____

_____

_____

_____

CHAPTER THREE
Conveying Character

This chapter explains how to build the basic "getting to know you" framework for your characters. You'll learn an indispensable trick for creating immediate reader buy-in. You'll understand how to use one or two details as a "gateway to characterization". Lastly, I'll show you how to scaffold of these skills to go even deeper into characterization.

In the last chapter, you identified the primary emotion of the character. That emotion sets the tone for the entire novel. It helps the reader dive into your story and embrace the mood that you're creating. Great writers always begin their novels with an emotional charge that hooks the reader. Though you generate that kind of charge through action, the effect is more profound if you hook your reader through the character right at the beginning. With the possible exception of *Dinotopia*—which was an extravaganza of setting—readers fall in love with characters.

Getting To Know Your Character

Before readers can fall in love with a character, they have to get to know the character on a purely practical level. Forget adjectives, flowery language and complex sentences for the moment. We're going to focus on character data.

Between your character opening and the end of Chapter 1, a few things must take place in order for you to have a cohesive scene. We dealt with the basics in character introduction, and now we'll explore what happens next.

Your first scene may include only a few characters. You introduce them and take the reader through the basics. In between that introduction and the end of the scene, setting and plot are introduced. There's an inciting incident and a transition to guide the reader expectation into the next scene. In the midst of all of this, you still have to deal with fleshing out your characters.

Within the first chapter, you'll discuss:

- Who your character is on a purely professional practical level
- Where is the character and why is he there?
- What activity or event is the character is engaged in.
- The characters' relationships to one another
- And you'll reveal the first small-scale character goal.

For this section, I'll use Katniss Everdeen again. In the first chapter of *The Hunger Games,* the reader finds out who Katniss is: the oldest daughter and the primary provider for the family. We find out where the character is and why: she lives in a house at the edge of the Seam in District 12. We learn what Katniss is doing that day and why: she's defying the law to hunt for food. The reader learns of the character relationships: sister Prim, Gale and mother are introduced. Lastly, we discover the small-scale character goal: she's protecting Prim from being chosen in the Hunger Games.

Quick Write First

You'll do the same for your characters as you introduce them in Chapter One. Even if you think you already know the answers to the bulleted list above, stop and write it out. This kind of logical, practical information can be offered in the most straightforward and practical way. Don't agonize over language. Get the foundation laid first before you start layering with language.

You will find that the more facts and hard data you compile on your character, the easier it becomes to actually write. Writers who struggle with openings are often forced to rewrite the opening because the character and the story evolved over the course of the novel. This is to be expected, but the process moves much more quickly and painlessly if you know as much as possible about the character from the outset.

Character Corroboration

There is one surefire way to hook the reader right from Chapter 1. It has nothing to do with fireworks or battlefield scenes. In order to convince a reader to follow you into the story, you must make her believe that the main character is worth knowing. One of the best and easiest ways to achieve this is through 'corroboration.'

By 'corroboration,' I mean validation and verification of your character. You may never have noticed, but great writers do this all the time. In *Harry Potter*, for example, the reader could see that Harry was a decent person who'd been beaten down by unpleasant people. He lived under the stairs and tried to get along as best he could. In fact, his restraint seemed quite noble at times. It was Hagrid's arrival and his response to Harry's plight that provided corroboration for Harry. "Yes," the reader said, "This boy is as decent and obliging as the text says he is. Let's get on with the story!"

This short, critical writing directive—more than any other I can add for character introduction—creates reader rapport and gets the ball rolling. As you introduce your main character, identify her emotional landscape and begin the action of the story, button up the introduction with corroboration from one or more characters in the scene. Let them validate your main character in a specific and credible way. Even something as simple as this: "Randoll knew that Callie was the most competent private investigator in Texas." (corroboration) "She'd not only behaved in the most scrupulous manner, but she'd solved at least two cases that had confounded more seasoned and experienced PIs with twice the manpower and resources." (specific details).

Without that corroboration, reader buy-in is a slower process with an uncertain outcome. Use other characters to endorse your main character in the first few pages. The reader will believe the assessments of other characters unless and until proven otherwise. Have a look at how Sir Arthur Conan Doyle uses corroboration in this excerpt:

"When I glance over my notes and records of the Sherlock Holmes cases between the years '82 and '90, I am faced by so many which present strange and interesting features that it is no easy matter to know which to choose and which to leave. Some, however, have already gained publicity through the papers, and others have not offered a field for those peculiar qualities which my friend possessed in so high a degree, and which it is the object of these papers to illustrate. Some, too, have baffled his analytical skill, and would be, as narratives, beginnings without an ending, while others have been but partially cleared up, and have their explanations founded rather upon conjecture and surmise than on that absolute logical proof which was so dear to him. There is, however, one of these last which was so remarkable in its details and so startling in its results that I am tempted to give some account of it in spite of the fact that there are points in connection with it which never have been, and probably never will be, entirely cleared up."

Arthur Conan Doyle. *The Adventures of Sherlock Holmes*

Describing Emotion

It's worthwhile to do a quick study of images that portray the emotion(s) you want to create so that you can isolate the visual cues that help explain that emotion through text. Then branch out from there and consider how other characters respond to that emotion. Use the responses and observations of other characters to loop back around to the emotion you're highlighting. Here's a simple example from Sherlock Holmes to get you started:

Classic Fiction

> *"The portly client puffed out his chest with an appearance of some little pride and pulled a dirty and wrinkled newspaper from the inside pocket of his greatcoat. As he glanced down the advertisement column, with his head thrust forward and the paper flattened out upon his knee, I took a good look at the man and endeavoured, after the fashion of my companion, to read the indications which might be presented by his dress or appearance. I did not gain very much, however, by my inspection. Our visitor bore every mark of being an average commonplace British tradesman, obese, pompous, and slow. He wore rather baggy grey shepherd's check trousers, a not over-clean black frock-coat, unbuttoned in the front, and a drab waistcoat with a heavy brassy Albert chain, and a square pierced bit of metal dangling down as an ornament. A frayed top-hat and a faded brown overcoat with a wrinkled velvet collar lay upon a chair beside him. Altogether, look as I would, there was nothing remarkable about the man save his blazing red head, and the expression of extreme chagrin and discontent upon his features."*
>
> Arthur Conan Doyle. *The Adventures of Sherlock Holmes*

- *Body Type:* Watson, then narrating, describes the man immediately as "portly" and follows that description up a sentence or two later with a less generous assessment of "obese."

- *Clothing:* In this passage, clothes revealed the man's social class, "a commonplace British tradesman." His outward appearance also gives cues as to what kind of a person he is: he is not quite clean, somewhat wrinkled and a little frayed.

- *Face & Emotional State:* Doyle ends with the description of his hair and face *because that detail of hair color, red, will feature importantly in the plot.* Again, <u>add details that reveal character and connect to plot.</u> Doyle ends with the description of the man's emotional state because that is the thread that will pull through to the next paragraph. He wants to make it obvious that the man is there because something has gone wrong.

- *Why It Works:* Doyle layers in adjectives here, but doesn't spin them all together. Instead, he parses them out in general terms first, "portly," and then adds the more specific adjective, "obese." Rather than resorting to another description of weight, Doyle focuses on the physical manifestations that readers would commonly associate with well-nourished men at the turn of the century in London, "pompous and slow."

- *Possibilities:* The value of character description like the one above lies in how you reveal the inner life of the character and then tie it back into plot.

FWM: Talvert Ferrara

"Talvert Ferrara was a solidly built man in his early thirties with the slight lines of experience just beginning to form on a handsome face. His thick brown hair pulled back into a short ponytail, his face handsome and tanned with the square jaw of a man who'd spent years in the company of other hard men. He carried himself like he'd once been a soldier. Even easy and relaxed as he was then, sunk into his leather office chair with one foot crossed over his knee, he gave the impression of being poised for action. The small gentle tapping of the pencil on the top of his thigh betrayed a line of muscle, a swell of sinew from years of training. He received the two men in his office, pointing to the chairs across the desk, and offered them a glass of scotch, but declined to take one for himself.

"Never developed a taste for it," he said with a smile."

Fiction Writing Maps: A Step-By-Step Guide To Characters

- *Body Type:* I've presented Talvert's body type in keeping with his military background and the work I need his character to do in the novel. I make certain throughout the novel to have him move in ways that reveal his military background.

- *Hair & Face:* I gave Talvert a blonde ponytail, a tanned face and some slight lines to show that he doesn't fall into the typical "professional" category and that he has some life experience.

- *Emotional State:* I've presented Talvert as "easy and relaxed" in a career setting. I added pencil tapping to show that he was on alert. The character Cal keeps in her hair, and I will use it in future scenes to draw these characters together.

- *Why It Works:* Although this is not as clean and precise as I would have liked, I was able to pull it together relatively quickly. I can always come back to it and revise it later.

- *Possibilities:* These kinds of character introductions are a nice way to give a basic overview of the character. This allows you a breathing space to quickly introduce characters when it's important to dive right into plot. Remember, quick introductions allow you to parse out details of a character bit by bit, which is much more satisfying that an infodump.

I provided this example from Sherlock Holmes because it introduces a key word that I wanted to highlight: "manner." When bringing characters onto the proverbial stage for the first time, think about their overall "manner."

"Manner" is a word that encompasses an enormous amount of information concerning character. Describing a character by "manner" allows the writer to import all of the corresponding details that accompany that "manner." For example, if a character has the manner of a Duke, that automatically generates details for the reader. More importantly, these are details that you don't have to convey—they come piggybacking along with the word. With thousands of examples of "manner' throughout literature, start thinking about the manner of your character and what specific language you could use to convey deeper characterization with just one or two words.

Classic Fiction

> "The man who entered was a sturdy, middle-sized fellow, some thirty years of age, clean-shaven, and sallow-skinned, with a bland, insinuating manner, and a pair of wonderfully sharp and penetrating grey eyes. He shot a questioning glance at each of us, placed his shiny top-hat upon the sideboard, and with a slight bow sidled down into the nearest chair."
>
> Arthur Conan Doyle. *The Adventures of Sherlock Holmes*

- *Body Type:* Sturdy and middle-sized is another example of a quick, general illustration of body type. It gives the reader just enough information to pencil an outline of the man.

- *Face & Eyes:* Doyle details this Character a bit further with references to his sallowness. He adds a tinge of perspicacity to the sketch with a "pair of wonderfully sharp and penetrating grey eyes."

- *Emotional State:* Doyle chooses the word "bland" to describe the client's manner in a wonderfully simple echo of the man's physical appearance. The "questioning" look and "sharply penetrating eyes" all hint at the man's emotional state without ever explicitly revealing it.

- *Why It Works:* After Doyle briefly describes the man, he sets the stage for the tone of the meeting. The man "shot a questioning glance" at Holmes and Watson. That's all it took to create tension and a hint of uncertainty to use as a pivot point into plot.

- *Possibilities:* See Sir Arthur Conan Doyle for more examples of these quick character sketches. They are so wickedly simple that you can use them anywhere as "stand-alone" descriptions or "openers" for parsing details and coming back to add layers.

FWM: Tocapo

"The man they called Tocapo entered the room, pausing at the door when his eyes fell on Calendar standing across the room. He was a tall, lean man with a shock of ginger hair combed boldly back from his face and a full beard trimmed closely around a small, perfectly formed mouth. A long white linen tunic hung over darker linen pants that might have been in fashion that week or a thousand years ago. Calendar watched him cross the room, walking with the restrained, measured step of a well-fed mountain lion.

He stopped directly in front of her and waited, allowing her to study him. The corner of his mouth bracketed into an indulgent smile and one almost blond brow raised slightly in amusement. He could not have been more than forty years old, Calendar thought, from the lines that crossed his forehead and settled at the corners of his mouth, yet his piercing blue eyes seemed older—almost ancient. The hand at his side twitched as if he'd had his fill of being watched and was ready to swat her out of existence."

Fiction Writing Maps: A Step-By-Step Guide To Characters

- *Body Type:* Since Tocapo probably won't feature much in the story, I've stuck to a general description of a "tall, lean man."

- *Face & Eyes:* I spent more area on his hair, face and eyes than anywhere else because the background material that I'll present at a later plot point is critical to this description.

- *Why It Works:* While this works well enough as a quick sketch, I realize that I can't really "see" this character definitively. I'll need to come back to this Character Map and work on finding the precise detail that will make him more realistic. That might not come from physical description, which is why I chose to keep moving forward.

Scaffolding Off Physical Traits

> *Use a physical trait as a gateway to describe your character's manner or emotional state. Keep the connection clear and concise.*

Good writers use physical traits as more than stand-alone descriptors. The lines on a character's face and the graying hair didn't just appear one day, but were the effect of specific choices, emotions and decisions. While it's essential for the reader to be able to visualize your characters, it's even more important for the reader to understand what life your character has lived and what choices he made that created the person he became.

As in real life, the inner landscape of a person is often reflected on the outside. So, latching onto key features is a good way to dig deeper into your character and uncover who he really is. For these examples, I'll spotlight one feature to use as a gateway for deeper characterization.

Keep in mind that the feature should run parallel to the inner dynamic you're exploring. A furrow between someone's eyebrows is usually indicative of deep thought, focused work or something along similar lines. Don't fight to tie it into something incongruous or random, but choose the features that allow an easy back and forth flow of information that you would expect to see if you were sitting across from your character.

FWM: Catherine Coullder

"Catherine Coullder had a chin reminiscent of Winston Churchill. She held it with the same clenching of the right teeth that caused her cheek to protrude in a slightly asymmetrical scowl of perpetual disturbance even when nothing was amiss. As the undisputed leader of the neighborhood that stretched from Congress Street to Convent Street and from Halepeska's Bakery to the bank, she ruled like Churchill, too. If someone stepped far enough out of line morals and good manners to merit her attention, they'd join the list unhappy people who'd endured a public thrashing that ruined their reputation among scoundrels and God fearing Christians alike. This morning, her plump cheek was florid and her brow knit together in an expression that made clear someone else was soon to be added to that list."

Fiction Writing Maps: A Step-By-Step Guide To Characters

Conveying Character

Step 1: What is your character's primary emotion? What does it look like when these reactions register in a character's face? What's the physical reaction? Is there a corresponding visceral reaction? Does it show or is it suppressed? Why? How do these responses affect what's going on in the setting? Write those out now in complete, unedited thoughts.

_____

_____

_____

_____

_____

_____

Step 2: Write out the answers to the following questions as if you were writing them into the novel. This not only saves a step, but it brings you immediately into the world of your novel as you write. Don't get wrapped up in language, but keep the answers simple and straightforward: Who your character is on a purely professional practical level? Where is the character and why is he there? What activity or event is he engaged in? Give a simple recitation of the relationships of the characters featured as they appear in Chapter 1. Reveal the first small-scale character goal. Write those out now in complete, unedited thoughts.

_____

_____

_____

_____

_____

_____

Step 3: What specific feature can you use as a gateway to show your character's physical appeal, trustworthiness, competence and social standing to the reader? Can you connect it back to an anecdote from your character's past or through exposition to anchor it more meaningfully in the novel? Can you tie it into a facial expression, a habit or her emotional state? Write those out in complete, unedited, thoughts

_____

_____

_____

_____

_____

_____

Step 4: Can you overlap any of the previous threads to zoom in on the nitty gritty of who your character is? Such as facial features, body language or an anecdote to support her emotional state? Write those out now in complete, unedited thoughts.

_____

_____

_____

_____

_____

Step 5: Choose one bit of physical description to use as a gateway to deeper characterization. Choose a characteristic that is central to your character's story. Show the physical feature in action on your character. Connect it back to an event or memory directly. Then circle back to the present moment in which your character is engaged and make that physical trait disclose some key insight that your reader MUST know in order for the plot to move forward. Write those out now in complete, unedited thoughts.

_____

_____

_____

_____

_____

CHAPTER FOUR
Motivating & Activating the Character

Learn how to bring your character to life and create an immediate bond with the reader by zeroing in on your character's firmly held belief, unwavering goal or deepest fear.

Motivation is the electrical charge that brings a character to life. Yet, even after reading fifty books that deal with the topic either as the central topic or as only a section, it took me a long time to pin down how the very abstract idea of character motivation translates into the process of building a character. Only after studying chapter openings across every genre did I finally nail it down. And once I unearthed this gem, the full force of its significance took shape.

Authors create brilliant characters by doing one critically important: they introduce a person, a thing or an idea about which the character cares very deeply *right away*. The sooner you can do this—but do it organically and meaningfully in the story—the better.

Activating Character

This is often just a short, succinct passage as the novel opens so don't make it into a long, elaborate explanation. After all, you wouldn't (I presume) bare your soul to a complete stranger and tell them every intimate detail about your deepest fears and failings? If you answered, "yes," then consider making your character a drunk who can't help but unload on a stranger in a bar. For the rest of you, take comfort in keeping this passage to its bare minimum.

Done correctly, it should evoke intense and specific feelings in the character (and reader). You've seen this at play in every major character in *Game of Thrones* and in characters like Tris Prior in *Divergent*. Wanting, needing, yearning and fearing lie at the heart of character motivation. Your character's desire operates like a tuning fork. Once struck, it will trigger a calculated feeling in your reader and tug their heartstrings *in the direction of your character's hopes and dreams.* Focus not on elegant language, but on concise, blisteringly real impulse and you're assured reader buy-in. In practical terms, it looks something like this in text:

Classic Fiction

"Oh, I can carry it," the child responded cheerfully. "It isn't heavy. I've got all my worldly goods in it, but it isn't heavy. And if it isn't carried in just a certain way the handle pulls out—so I'd better keep it because I know the exact knack of it. It's an extremely old carpet-bag. Oh, I'm very glad you've come, even if it would have been nice to sleep in a wild cherry-tree. We've got to drive a long piece, haven't we? Mrs. Spencer said it was eight miles. I'm glad because I love driving. Oh, it seems so wonderful that I'm going to live with you and belong to you. I've never belonged to anybody—not really. But the asylum was the worst. I've only been in it four months, but that was enough. I don't suppose you ever were an orphan in an asylum, so you can't possibly understand what it is like. It's worse than anything you could imagine. Mrs. Spencer said it was wicked of me to talk like that, but I didn't mean to be wicked. It's so easy to be wicked without knowing it, isn't it? They were good, you know—the asylum people. But there is so little scope for the imagination in an asylum—only just in the other orphans. It was pretty interesting to imagine things about them—to imagine that perhaps the girl who sat next to you was really the daughter of a belted earl, who had been stolen away from her parents in her infancy by a cruel nurse who died before she could confess. I used to lie awake at nights and imagine things like that, because I didn't have time in the day. I guess that's why I'm so thin—I am dreadful thin, ain't I? There isn't a pick on my bones. I do love to imagine I'm nice and plump, with dimples in my elbows."

L. M. Montgomery. *Anne of Green Gables*

Classic Fiction

"With a sigh of rapture she relapsed into silence. Matthew stirred uneasily. He felt glad that it would be Marilla and not he who would have to tell this waif of the world that the home she longed for was not to be hers after all. They drove over Lynde's Hollow, where it was already quite dark, but not so dark that Mrs. Rachel could not see them from her window vantage, and up the hill and into the long lane of Green Gables. By the time they arrived at the house Matthew was shrinking from the approaching revelation with an energy he did not understand. It was not of Marilla or himself he was thinking of the trouble this mistake was probably going to make for them, but of the child's disappointment. When he thought of that rapt light being quenched in her eyes he had an uncomfortable feeling that he was going to assist at murdering something — much the same feeling that came over him when he had to kill a lamb or calf or any other innocent little creature."

L. M. Montgomery. *Anne of Green Gables*

FWM: Sio

> *"Sio, looked up, hands coated with the colored icing, to see the school children lining up just outside the bistro door, and she wondered if the day would ever come when she would look out to see her own children running through those doors. Would there be a time when a blond pony-tailed girl or a smaller version of Charles would tumble in pink-cheeked and ready for a kiss, a cookie and a glass of lemonade? She looked forward to the familiar soft, sweaty smell of the playground and gap-toothed smiles. Her heart contracted at the sight of those wide open, grateful faces peering in through the window as they waited for her to pass out the leftover sugar cookies. What if she was consigned to spending her entire life loving other people's children and never having any of her own? Her stomach lurched at the painful thought. 'It would happen. It would happen,' she told herself."*
>
> *Fiction Writing Maps: A Step-By-Step Guide To Characters*

As you begin to think about how to motivate your character, give some thought to Maslow's hierarchy of needs. If you're unfamiliar with it, have a look at The Fiction Writing Maps Blog to explore Maslow's Hierarchy of Needs.

Succinctly put, Maslow theorized that human needs are arranged in a hierarchy. The five-stage model Maslow created explains how human needs are organized along a stratified structure from biological needs to self-actualization needs.

Maslow's Hierarchy

- Biological and Physiological needs - air, food, drink, shelter, warmth, sex, sleep.

- Safety needs - protection from elements, security, order, law, stability, freedom from fear.

- Love and belongingness needs - friendship, intimacy, trust and acceptance, receiving and giving affection and love. Affiliating, being part of a group (family, friends, work).

- Esteem needs - achievement, mastery, independence, status, dominance, prestige, self-respect, respect from others.

- Self-Actualization needs - realizing personal potential, self-fulfillment, seeking personal growth and peak experiences.

Think back to *The Hunger Games* for a perfect literary example of Maslow's hierarchy in fiction. Suzanne Collins began the series with a hungry and desperate cast of characters. Readers were instantly concerned for the safety of Katniss, and this fear, along with her love for her family, drew the readers into the story.

Throughout the novel, Collins moves Katniss up and down this hierarchy of need. Katniss fights for survival, forges alliances and friendships, gains respect from her peers and looks ahead to the future she wants to create. Notice, that this isn't always a steady climb up the pyramid. The nature of conflict is that characters slip, dust themselves, learn something important and begin to climb again.

For another example of Maslow's hierarchy of needs, have a look at Clint's excerpt as he introduces the character of Bilal.

> *"He was asleep, locked in the recurring dream that had haunted him the past few nights. He stood at the edge of the village to see his father kneeling in the middle of the road, his back to Bilal. A line of tanks approached, kicking up clouds of dust as they rolled into the village. Each night, Bilal began the sprint to the road earlier in the dream than the night before. He felt the muscles bunch in his legs, pushed off at an even faster pace than the night before, but felt the same growing dread. He was trapped in the surreal dichotomy of the dream world where arms and legs pumped in furious, forward motion, but the quicksand of failure held him fast. Bilal reached out, shouting across the space that separated his father from him. The old man turned and smiled at Bilal as if he was oblivious to the line of tanks bearing down on him. His father mouthed one word.....'Run.'"*
>
> Clint Wilson. *On The Pharm*

The Greatest Is Love

There is only one human emotion which never fails to draw readers into a story—Love. It can take many forms, running from compassionate love to intensity bordering on jealousy. However, love is the breath that animates fictional characters, and humans beings are universally attracted to the resonance of that emotion. Writers who depict this emotion in the relationships of their characters create huge followings. When you can write love in a way that feels authentic, readers fall in love, too.

Make your characters love something or someone—more than themselves—and they will walk right off the page. Activating the character and providing Motivation work hand-in-hand. Center your character's motivation in love and you can't go too far wrong. I'll give a passage here from one of the most popular books of all time to illustrate this point:

Classic Fiction

> *"She threw her arms around the Lion's neck and kissed him, patting his big head tenderly. Then she kissed the Tin Woodman, who was weeping in a way most dangerous to his joints. But she hugged the soft, stuffed body of the Scarecrow in her arms instead of kissing his painted face, and found she was crying herself at this sorrowful parting from her loving comrades. Glinda the Good stepped down from her ruby throne to give the little girl a good-bye kiss, and Dorothy thanked her for all the kindness she had shown to her friends and herself. Dorothy now took Toto up solemnly in her arms, and having said one last good-bye she clapped the heels of her shoes together three times, saying: "Take me home to Aunt Em!"*
>
> L. Frank Baum. *The Wonderful Wizard of Oz*

Fear Works, Too

Love is not the only tool for activating characters. On the other side of Maslow's scale, fear also works to galvanize a character. Because fear resonates in that primal place at the lowest rung of Maslow, it engages readers intensely. In fact, this is why the opening of The Hunger Games played so well. The dread we felt for Katniss was made all the more poignant because of the love she felt for her sister. Collins then used fear to activate the character of Katniss. From there, she began a slow and steady drip of danger that ratcheted up the intensity of the novel. In that first chapter of The Hunger Games, we saw character activation and motivation in its highest form.

Motivating & Activating the Character

Step 1: What motivates your reader demographic? Spend some time making a list of the most—and least—common motivations. Use Maslow's hierarchy of needs to think about how you might move your character from one rung to another as the plot unfolds. Write those out now in complete, unedited thoughts.

_____

_____

_____

_____

_____

Step 2: Can you focus on a clear, powerful motivating factor to incorporate in the first chapter? Can you draw the tension of that motivation to include another character or characters? What would the sequel to that tension look like? Write those out now in complete, unedited thoughts

_____

_____

_____

_____

_____

Step 3: Which of your character's fears paralyze him? Which of his beliefs reinforce that fear? What action will your character have to take to move past his fear? Write those out now in complete, unedited thoughts.

Step 4: Who or what does your character love more than himself? Can you chart out the What, Why, Where, When and How behind that love? Give your character more than feelings; provide a those feelings with purpose by providing a story that explains those feelings. Why does your character love this person, place or idea? What would challenge that love? What if that almost happened? Can you think of a way to bring that love close to disaster without smashing it entirely? Write those out now in complete, unedited thoughts.

CHAPTER FIVE

A New Spin on Archetypes

> In this chapter, I'll explain how to use Jung's Archetypes as a starting point for creating a unique Archetype for your main character. Combine archetypes or crisscross traits to give both your characters and the plot intriguing nuances.

Like it or not, human beings categorize everything-especially people. I don't use the term in a "categorize" in a negative way; I use it to describe the logistics of a decision-making process that helps us develop our response to new people. When we meet someone new, the first thing we try to establish is what "kind of person" they are. Are they good or bad, kind or mean-spirited, trustworthy or corrupt? Our initial opinion helps frame a concept of that person that will likely stick.

Your readers go through this process when you introduce a character.

One of your first responsibilities is to help the reader plop your characters into a "category." This is the only way that a reader can settle into the story and try to make sense of the plot as it unfolds. Readers must be able to identify the good guys from the bad guys and determine where characters fit into the social construct of your novel.

In a very literal sense, readers rely on archetypes to help classify characters. This doesn't mean that your characters have to fall into the same, stale groupings. You can combine archetypes to create new dimensions, writing damsel-in-distress villains and sidekick mentors. Just make sure that readers know where your characters fall on a general scale as you begin to develop the story.

Spinning Your Archetype

Carl Jung first applied the term 'archetypes' to writing when he posited that there were universally understood patterns in literature that crossed cultural and historical boundaries. Jung detailed this list of archetypes and provided descriptions for each of their literary journeys. Archetypes—as I discuss them here—are characters depicted in literature who share a similar structure and function that allows readers to easily categorize them.

For example, the Hero and the Temptress conjure up immediate images for readers. We can point to countless examples in literature and film for both of those archetypes. They're so familiar that we know precisely what to expect of their roles within the plot structure. And therein lies the problem.

Writers have used Jung's work to build their cast and flesh out the roles for each character. Based on the archetype, readers know what to expect from the character, and thus, the story. But rather than rely solely on archetypes to guide character

JACKIE ST. JAMES

creation, I suggest using it as a starting point to choose specific traits that your character will need to help propel the plot forward.

So how does a writer push the boundaries of archetype to develop new iterations while still retaining enough of Jung's traits to make the archetypes familiar?

Mix It Up

Rather than having characters conform to one archetype, explore what traits your character might use if you stole from another archetype. *The Wizard of Oz*, for example, did this beautifully. L. Frank Baum added 'The Friendly Beast' to the group of 'Hunting Companions,' shifting the archetype just enough to add conflict and excitement to the story structure. Glenda the Good was a cross between Mentor & Guardian. While these two archetypes are not so different in purpose, it did give the character added weight within the story.

Scaffolding off this concept, you can do the same with your own characters. Crisscross traits between archetypes to create 'Damsels in Distress' who become 'Mentors' or 'Initiates' who become 'Threshold Guardians.' Spend some time mapping out what traits your character needs to help do the work of the plot. What weaknesses or failings could you weave into the mix that would challenge your character? Think about how closely aligned your hero and villain are and look for a common thread between the two that might bend towards an archetype you hadn't considered.

Katniss Everdeen is another modern example of this archetypal spin. Her character traits combine the warrior, the guardian, the rebel and the hero.

70

Interestingly enough, she also eschews the more common path of so many modern heroines and doesn't fall into the arms of the love interest for the 'happily ever after' ending. Could you combine character archetypes to modify reader expectations?

Stretch The Boundaries

This technique actually mimics reality rather than stretching the boundaries of truth. There are not any of us who walk precisely along the archetypal lines as they're mapped out by Jung. The people you know are mixtures of Hero and Damsel-In-Distress, and Mentors are sometimes Gatekeepers and Hermits. These are the inconsistencies and anomalies that make people interesting. They make your characters more interesting as well. How can you crisscross Archetypes to create a more realistic, vibrant character? Building a new iteration lets you imagine intriguing nuances that add light, shadow and dimension to your characters.

Through your work in the previous chapter you should have a clear paragraph that details what *kind* of person your character is and what led you to that conclusion. You should also have an idea of what kind of villain she would make. Now it's time to dig through that writing and look for different archetypes that incorporate those threads and add new dimensions to the character.

Hero or Villain?

A quick word here about the opposing nature of Archetypes. In the end, heroes and villains are two sides of the same coin. Given minor deviations of circumstances, a villain could be a hero—a hero could become villainous. Keep that nugget of truth in mind as you craft your characters because characters are often as much a result of what they choose to avoid as what they choose to embrace. Where does your character draw the moral and ethical line? How does that compare and contrast with the villain? In what ways are they alike? These are all good questions to explore as you draft these characters.

Walking the fine line in between for both hero and villain creates tension in the plot. Look at your hero's greatest strength—then ask yourself what made him want to take up the sword? If you took all of the loving-kindness out of him, what might he do with that power? Explore that. Write backstory around that. This exercise can also help you pinpoint your character's weakness. When you find that chink in a character's armor, you've found another point of tension to use in the plot. What one thing would push your hero over the edge? Perhaps an old grudge still lies festering, and it's the one and only weakness in an otherwise stalwart and noble hero. There's your point of tension to explore and exploit. When you've completed this exercise for your hero, do the same for your villain. That's where character creation becomes even more interesting.

To illustrate this point in film, I'll use the Sylvester Stallone movie, Rocky III:

The movie opens on Rocky Balboa living a comfortable, successful life years after winning the heavyweight championship.

In fact, Rocky has become downright complacent in the aftermath of victory.

By contrast, "Clubber" Lang (played by Mr. T), is driven to train with a single-minded determination that we haven't seen since we watched a younger, less civilized Rocky rise to his power in the first installment.

Looking at Lang, minus the 'lens' of a villain, we see a vigorous, focused fighter who doesn't back down from a challenge and puts in the grueling work that fuels a win.

Moreover, he's alone.

While Rocky has a family, a multi-million dollar home and the admiration of the world, Lang works out in a dingy gym and sleeps in a one-bedroom dive. And dreams of glory.

In a flipped version of this story, Lang might be the underdog, the lonely, unlikely hero. But we are viewing through the director's lens and he is telling us who the hero is in this version.

Tragically, Rocky loses his first fight.

However, two traits save Rocky in the aftermath of his defeat, neither of which are characteristics that people generally use to describe Rocky Balboa: discernment and humility.

Rocky finally sees the problem clearly and takes the appropriate steps towards a solution.

When we speak of archetypes, we know that certain character traits travel with each archetype. As you plan your character, think back to the traits that you listed in Chapter 1 to describe her. These core beliefs will guide your character's decisions and actions. Your character might wander away from those beliefs for a while—as Rocky did—but he must come back to those threads to complete the loop of story.

Here's what happened with Rocky:

> *In a beautifully orchestrated ending, Rocky returns to the roots of his first victory. He has the humility to strip away the glamorous life he's won and get back to his roots. He joins Lang on a grittier, harder field of training. There, villain and hero meet again. One wins and one loses. Rocky returns triumphantly to the roots of his victory and the arc of change is complete.*

A New Spin on Archetypes

Step 1: Look through Character Archetypes to choose a few that fit with your character. Write down why each trait fits in complete, unedited thoughts

_____

_____

_____

_____

_____

Step 2: Now brainstorm secondary traits that might fit your character. How might you explain where those traits came from and turn that history into a segment of story? Write down why each trait fits in complete, unedited thoughts

_____

_____

_____

_____

_____

Step 3: Explore how close you can get to more villainous traits. Does that uncover any secondary archetype that might fit your character? Write this down in complete, unedited thoughts.

_____

_____

_____

_____

_____

Step 4: Explain in narrative form why those archetypes apply to your character. Use explicit events from the past, vignettes or memories from other characters to elaborate. In order to peg that personality trait to your character, ask yourself, "What makes [her] a Gatekeeper, Companion, Bandit?" Write with the goal of adding this narrative segment to your story. Don't' stop to edit or second-guess your writing.

_____

_____

_____

_____

_____

CHAPTER SIX
Creating History & Parsing Backstory

In this chapter, you'll discover how to use the past to broaden the scale of your story. We'll reveal a writing technique that parses character backstories to create forward momentum and look at how authors use past events and history to create depth with the illusory passage of time.

Thus far, we've explored the straight road of creating and writing characters. In this section, we switch course to explore a different landscape of The Map. The best way to illustrate the use of history within a novel is by comparison. If the novel is a pool of water, 'history' is each bit of information from the collective pasts of the characters that acts like a pebble tossed into the water. If the history you've designed is sparse and the pool is shallow, your story lacks scope. This is not necessarily a bad thing. Some stories aren't designed to be epic works. However, notice that the masterpieces such as *Dune* have layer upon layer of history weaved throughout the story. These are not puddles of prose. Authors like Herbert and George R. R. Martin, focus their writing lenses far back in time to design elaborate, extravagant histories within their novels. This technique creates a wider, deeper expanse into which the author can toss a million pebbles of information.

Designing history and weaving it into your novel does something more than simply adding more layers of complexity and interest to the story. This is the purpose of building history within the novel. History is the foundation upon which an author constructs the illusion of time, and that illusion adds texture and richness to the characters. This is the purpose of discussing history as you craft your characters.

Tolkien's legendary novel, *Lord of The Rings*, offers the best example for purposes of illustration. Tolkien developed a rich and complex past for his individual characters, and also for the races to which they belong. The Elves, for example, were designed with superb detail that included everything from their origins and language to their wars and prophecies. The same can be said for the Dwarves and the Orcs.

This use of history gives characters a tribe, an identify and a shared past. When the reader has a fundamental understanding of the past within the story, they gain insight into character motivations and conflicts. This is the launching pad from which characters evolve.

Though you may not want to write an epic novel, it's still worthwhile to group your characters and create histories for those groups—even if they're brief. Give the reader a basic list comprised of Names, Houses, Religion, Culture, Family and

Alliances if you can. Including this kind of history will widen the vista and add substance and sweep to your story.

Building Backstory

Now that you have a basic character, an introduction and a starting point, it's time to give your character a backstory. Backstory works like a rear view mirror for the reader: it expands their field of vision and helps them navigate the road ahead as they keep track of what's behind them. Through backstory, readers learn to understand the character's present state of mind. It reveals the events of the past that made the character who he is today. These 'stories within the story' also help the reader predict what a character might do next. In this way, the writer can frame expectations and create tension when a character challenges those expectations.

Divulging a character's backstory shouldn't be a chronological dictation from start to finish. Character backstories become meaningful when details from the past appear sparingly over the course of the novel and are so subtle that the reader almost misses the intrusion of information onto the narrative. Backstory needs to be relevant to the immediate events of the story and to explain an action or event in the present moment that cannot be understood without access to the past. This is the function of backstory, and just as in architecture, "form follows function" in building the character.

One Piece At A Time

Parse backstory with the stinginess of a Kindergartener forced to hand out Halloween candy. Wait until the reader absolutely needs the fact that you are giving him in order for the plot to move forward. Then—and only then—give the smallest portion they need in order to move forward with the plot. Then stop abruptly. Rather than telling everything at once, you make them wait at the edge of resolution.

Leaving that gap has a twofold purpose. An abrupt end to the flow of information engage readers. When you pause in the middle of describing how your character was left as an infant on the church steps on Christmas Eve, you have the reader's attention. They want to know what happened. They need to know what happened. They're motivated to keep going, and this kind of reader engagement is what good writers yearn to achieve. If you spill the entire lot of information, the reader takes it without working for it. It cost them nothing to get it, and thus it has no meaning.

However, leaving the gap has a profound effect. It turns readers into sleuths. They think back through clues you've already given them to try to figure out what happened. Even when they have to put the book down, they're still thinking about where you stopped. When they pick the novel up again, they read furiously to find out how close the character came to death and who saved her life on Christmas Eve. Make backstory the treasure for which readers have to dig, and make that excavation vigorous and rewarding.

Now that you understand the role of history and backstory, let's look at how you can build those into your novel.

Anecdotes

Readers love characters with salacious pasts, romantic entanglements and old wounds. These gossipy chunks of story contribute to the central plot because they contain clues as to who your character is and why she behaves the way she does. They provide the reader with insight into the thoughts and actions of your character and guide expectations as the plot moves forward.

Anecdotes are a great vehicle for establishing that connection. They offer a layer of credibility since the information doesn't come directly from the author or the character herself, but from a third source. The brilliant part of this technique is that the character disclosing the anecdote may or may not be a reliable spokesperson—it doesn't matter. You can still use that character to reveal the anecdotal information.

Time Travel

As in history, the anecdote uses the passage of time as a tool. This is a little-used, but extraordinarily powerful device. Consider *The Hobbit* where Tolkien layers the story with anecdotes and songs to fashion luxurious histories for elves, men and hobbits. They have victories, epic losses, moments of personal weakness and catastrophic judgment that are recorded and handed down.

Tolkien weaves the past of this fictitious world like threads on a loom. He moves back and forth in time to grab a colorful piece of the past and tie it into the present. This technique adds weight and credibility to the story as the decisions of the characters during the present moment of the story often rely on untangling the past

81

or predicting the future. It's this concept of time that you want to isolate, utilize and highlight in your story. More than any other technique I've studied, this allows the reader to suspend disbelief and engage in the plot. When the characters believe enough in the past to apply it to the present moment or use it to plan for the future, you've done your work.

Classic Anecdote

This excerpt from _Pride and Prejudice_ illustrates an ingenious use of anecdote. The passage shows Mr. Darcy at a particularly vulnerable moment in the story. Here, he tells the story of Willoughby taking advantage of his sister's innocence to spirit her away in an attempt to marry her. It seems simple and is almost lost in the larger scope this brilliant novel. In this instance, Austen's genius masquerades as just another gem of writing. However, I argue that this letter is the pivot point upon which the entire novel hinges. It does the work of turning the plot within one short space.

Classic Fiction

"I must now mention a circumstance which I would wish to forget myself, and which no obligation less than the present should induce me to unfold to any human being. Having said thus much, I feel no doubt of your secrecy. My sister, who is more than ten years my junior, was left to the guardianship of my mother's nephew, Colonel Fitzwilliam, and myself. About a year ago, she was taken from school, and an establishment formed for her in London; and last summer she went with the lady who presided over it, to Ramsgate; and

> *thither also went Mr. Wickham, undoubtedly by design; for there proved to have been a prior acquaintance between him and Mrs. Younge, in whose character we were most unhappily deceived; and by her connivance and aid, he so far recommended himself to Georgiana, whose affectionate heart retained a strong impression of his kindness to her as a child, that she was persuaded to believe herself in love, and to consent to an elopement. She was then but fifteen, which must be her excuse; and after stating her imprudence, I am happy to add, that I owed the knowledge of it to herself."*
>
> Jane Austen. *Pride and Prejudice*

This anecdote within the letter not only gives us information about Darcy's past, but does something subtle and profound. Austen creates space from the teller—Darcy—to the readers—Elizabeth and the audience. This seems like a simple, commonplace technique. However, the story that Darcy tells is so personal and raw, and the telling of it is so out of character for the man, that it could not have been done any other way. The events regarding Georgiana's escapade were such a closely-guarded secret that the disclosure could only have come from Mr. Darcy. The letter provides a sense of distance and space, as letters and text messages often do. Darcy makes himself vulnerable, open again to being rebuffed and scorned. When he divulges Willoughby's salacious past, he opens up. It's a gutsy move from a man deeply in love. Pride and prejudice are pushed aside, and he emerges in all of his sensitivity and nobility.

The combination of anecdote and letter gives Elizabeth and the readers room to wriggle uncomfortably as Darcy tells the story. Recall the times that you've been on the receiving end of a text message about someone else's bad fortune that made you feel uncomfortable for them. Most likely, you were relieved to receive it as a message rather than to endure it in person. The use of the letter makes this situation less awkward for Elizabeth as well. This is a conversation that would have been impossible over tea.

The space Austen creates here with the letter is a masterpiece of psychology, storytelling and writing. Remember that the audience for this novel would have felt this embarrassment more keenly than modern day readers. This anecdote exposes a bad character, soothes Elizabeth's pain and reaches across the distance to bring Darcy and Elizabeth back together from the precipice of a tragic ending. Would that every lover's quarrel ended with such epic brilliance.

- *Anecdote:* This writing in the anecdote is also multi-layered. Austen uses syntax to give the writing a chopped, emotional feel. She includes only the most relevant details to spare Elizabeth's (and the reader's) more delicate sensibilities.
- *Why It Works:* One of the reasons that this passage works so well is because the character of Mr. Darcy has been so remote and cold that the reader hasn't had many real opportunities for insight into the man behind the social façade. More than any other excerpt within the novel, this one truly characterizes Darcy, and that's why readers love it.

Musings of Characters

We're moving away from history and anecdote to briefly explore another technique of incorporating the past into the novel. Some of the work done in the novel comes from the observations and musings of the characters. Between the words, actions, narrative and dialogue there are spaces of thoughts, observations and memories. Just like anecdotes and histories, these provide fertile ground for bringing pieces of the past into the present moment.

How do you write something as illusory as a thought and make it effective?

Like you and I, a character's brain activity isn't always anchored to the present or envisioning the future. Thoughts (both ours and the character's) rarely proceed in straight line from start to finish. There is a free-flow of activity that resembles a spider web more than a straight road. Has there ever been a time when you were speaking to someone and they switched topics so abruptly that you couldn't follow their line of thought? That is perhaps the best example to explain the technique for writing character musings.

An internal thinking pattern often begins with one idea. This might be a word, a person, an event, an action or a memory. Your brain latches onto it and explores it for a time. Inevitably, another thought occurs that pulls your attention away from the first thought. Your mind then leaps from the first idea to the next. As the brain explores ideas, we look for connections and search for other, related threads of meaning. You may even reach across space, subject and structure to another thought that is related only by the association you've created. For most people (I'm assuming), this is a normal, unstructured flow of thinking. So, it is for characters. This is how writers bring past to present, show motivation and establish character arcs.

The technique of weaving past, present and future is found in classic literature, but modern storytellers have distilled it down to a simple, effective system. While modern literature provides more explicit examples, it's difficult to find one that isn't copyrighted. I've included an example from classic fiction and illustrated it again with a unique piece of writing.

The key to mastering this technique is to begin with a clear focus of the point you want to achieve within the anecdote. Know your objective before you even begin to write. Know where your character's idea begins and where it will end. Decide what you're divulging and why. Explore your character's thinking pattern from start to finish. You might even use a thinking map to trace the initial idea to the last, building bubbles that show the nexus points and lines upon which you can explain the underlying reasoning. But plan it. Thinking one's own thoughts are difficult enough. Trying to follow the ruminations of a character whose thoughts don't follow a well-marked path is just annoying.

When you write a character's thoughts, try mimicking the web, but stay grounded in a logical flow. The web is a chaos of overlapping threads within a larger symmetry of design. The purpose of each individual thread is to capture an idea and lead to a pivotal point where another idea intersects. Eventually, all threads point back towards the middle, towards the point of origin. This is how a memory pattern for a character is designed.

The best examples of this writing technique are found in the brilliant novels of Louise Penny, which I highly recommend. I can't include them here because of copyright issues, but they are perfectly orchestrated writing loops that dive into the past, pull out clues and drive the plot forward. Each begin with one event, one idea or one visual. Then, like the web, Penny picks up another piece and walks the words to the next key bit of information. As she does this, she gives the reader wonderful, intimate glimpses into her characters. This technique is incredibly effective for introducing a cast of characters, and Louise Penny does it flawlessly.

As she finishes her character's examination of the moment or of the past, she inevitably circles back around to the inciting word, image, idea or observation that sparked the thought process. She ends where the character began. This is what I call "Writing in a Loop." It is effective because it does something very subtle and very cunning. It makes the reader trust the writer. People who read mysteries love a mystery, but they love closure twice as much. Writing in a loop mimics closure. It's a treat to use again and again to entice the reader on a small scale with an implied promise of fulfillment on a larger scale. The process is both satisfying and addicting—as her millions of readers can attest.

Let's explore these concepts in examples from both Classic Fiction and original examples.

Classic Fiction

> *"Go and dress, dear; you'll be late." "All right, mother—"She obeyed, but loitered disconsolately at the landing window. It faced north, so there was little view, and no view of the sky. Now, as in the winter, the pine-trees hung close to her eyes. One connected the landing window with depression. No definite problem menaced her, but she sighed to herself, "Oh, dear, what shall I do, what shall I do?" It seemed to her that everyone else was behaving very badly. And she ought not to have mentioned Miss Bartlett's letter. She must be more careful; her mother was rather inquisitive, and might have asked what it was about. Oh, dear, what should she do?— and then Freddy came bounding upstairs, and joined the ranks of the ill-behaved. "I say, those are topping people." "My dear baby, how tiresome you've been! You have no business to take them bathing in the Sacred Lake; it's*

much too public. It was all right for you but most awkward for everyone else. Do be more careful. You forget the place is growing half suburban." "I say, is anything on to-morrow week?" "Not that I know of." "Then I want to ask the Emersons up to Sunday tennis." "Oh, I wouldn't do that, Freddy, I wouldn't do that with all this muddle." "What's wrong with the court? They won't mind a bump or two, and I've ordered new balls." "I meant it's better not. I really mean it." He seized her by the elbows and humorously danced her up and down the passage. She pretended not to mind, but she could have screamed with temper. Cecil glanced at them as he proceeded to his toilet and they impeded Mary with her brood of hot-water cans. Then Mrs. Honeychurch opened her door and said: "Lucy, what a noise you're making! I have something to say to you. Did you say you had had a letter from Charlotte?" and Freddy ran away. "Yes. I really can't stop. I must dress too."

E. M. Forster. *A Room with a View*

FWM: Vignette

"Finally Calendar spoke. 'I know a back way around the railroad tracks.' She said it so casually that it took Carter a moment to process it. He stopped crying and looked up.

Her blue eyes met his, unwavering. Could she be suggesting what he thought? What eleven-year-old girl had that kind of courage?

The far corner of her right brow twitched up in a challenge that asked how far he would go to get Jasper back.

"It's through the woods. No one goes there. They just use it as a dump. It's littered with a bunch of old furniture and a rotted out car. We can sneak right up to the back of the house and no one will see us. "

Calendar imparted this bit of information as casually as if she was telling him the way to the snow cone stand rather than reciting the back way to the most dangerous house in town.

"If your dog's at Russell's house, we should be able to hear him bark."

He had been treading water, nearly drowning in grief. He felt his toes graze sand—felt the sandbar of hope.

They pedaled past the church, along trails in the woods that he hadn't even known were there. They ditched their bikes to walk the rest of the way and crawled the last few feet before coming to rest behind a blue plastic water barrel. And there they waited. It was the longest two minutes of his life. He heard snuffling and a bark from the other side of Russell's fence.

He'd brought Jasper home thanks to Calendar. Calendar had sprinted to the fence before he could speak, pried back one of the half-rotted slats and pulled Jasper from the mouth of Hell.

But it was what had happened the next day that left Carter stunned. Hearing sirens, he'd jumped on his bike and careened towards the wailing police cars and fire engines. He'd run headlong into Calendar, head down, pedaling furiously away from the commotion as if the Hounds of Hell were after her.

Carter thought back to that day as he saw the thin line of Calendar's eyebrow twitch up in unspoken challenge.

'I know a way into the compound,' she said.

How badly did he want to solve this mystery?"

FWM: Calendar McCrae

"Judge Hagler bent over the paper, drumming his beefy fingers in a quick staccato on the desktop as he squinted over the warrant.

Calendar's eyes drifted to the top of his head, resting on the peninsula of grey hair. She remembered the first time she sat in this chair and asked him to sign the papers that would make her an emancipated minor. He'd had a full head of salt and pepper hair then. She felt a pang of guilt for the stress she'd caused over the years, but not enough to stop her from doing what she came here to do.

JACKIE ST. JAMES

The drumming of his fingers stopped abruptly and Judge Hagler leaned back hard, the hinges of the chair squeaking in protest.

'Kid, you've asked me to sign some stupid shit before, but this one tops them all."

Calendar had prepared for this response.

'If you don't sign it, I'll go straight to the television stations, Roy. I'll post the video from the game cam to YouTube, promote it and this place will be packed with reporters, paparazzi and Feds. I'll say I tried... Russell tried...' she corrected, 'to get you to sign the warrant and you refused. You and I both know that something dangerous is going on in that compound. You have a duty—a responsibility—to the people of Edenburg to let Russell find out what it is.'

Haglar made a chucking noise of annoyance, pulled the handkerchief from his pocket and began daubing the sweat that had beaded at the top of his head.

'Russell isn't smart enough to find anything but the inside of a beer bottle, and half the time he can be counted on to screw that up, too. Cut the bullshit, Calendar. What do you think happened on that compound?'

'Please, Roy. Don't make me explain. You wouldn't understand it and you wouldn't believe me. Save us both the trouble and just trust me.'

Haglar reached out to beat another, faster rhythm on the side of his desk. Quickly, and without a word, he grabbed the pen, dashed off his signature and tossed the paper across the desk to Calendar.

'If this goes south, I'm throwing you to the wolves, kid.'

Breathing a sigh of relief, Calendar flashed him a smile.

'Would you really do that to the wolves?' "

Fiction Writing Maps: A Step-By-Step Guide To Characters

90

Quick Transitions

Getting to backstory is only a question of transitioning from the present to the past. This transition doesn't need to be a long, drawn out process. As with so many writing tasks, the simplest route is often the best route. Here's a quick example of a quick and easy transition into backstory from a work by Clint. Notice how it shifts in the space of two sentences from the present moment to an opening that allows the writer to dive into backstory.

> *"She had been getting bulletins all morning. Any normal person would buckle like a house of cards in a stiff breeze under the same amount of pressure, multi-tasking and split second decision making with such massive consequences at stake, but Toni Rudolph was not your average person."*
>
> Clint Wilson. *Total News Global*

Moving back into the present takes even less time as you can see in this other example from another work by Clint.

> *"Annika winced, suddenly pulled from her daydreams by the pinging completion of the software search. The white noise of electronics came rushing back as the printer whirred out the results of the program."*
>
> Clint Wilson. *On The Pharm*

Parsing History & Backstory

Step 1: Can you highlight one or two key traits your character exhibits that would be more practical if told from the point of view of another character? Consider choosing things that people don't discover about themselves. For instance, a character might be easygoing with everyone else, but harsh with a specific person because some incident in the past taught him he couldn't trust that person. It would then be another character's job to point this imbalance out. What anecdote could you create that would reveal—rather than tell—this trait? How will that trait tie into your character's arc of change? Write this down in complete, unedited thoughts.

_____

_____

_____

_____

_____

Step 2: Can you draw that anecdote out to include other characters at later parts in the story who can corroborate or contradict the anecdote? What would those interactions look like and how would they affect your character's credibility? Where do each of those interaction appear in the plot of your story? Place them there now. Write down where you might turn those bits into a segment of story in complete, unedited thoughts

_____

_____

_____

_____

_____

Step 3: Think about the words you'll use to build the illusion of passing time. Sentence starters like "I was an innocent in those days. Inclined to believe that everything I heard from my parents was fact. [Insert the anecdote here. Then gradually ease back into the present with the continuation that come next] But experience and failure had guided me to another place. Now I believe absolutely nothing."

Along which key traits will your character arc? Name them. Create anecdote(s) to illustrate that trait with perfect clarity. Practice moving back and forth through time as you weave the thread of the past into the present. Write this down in complete, unedited thoughts and place them in your story.

_____

_____

_____

_____

_____

CHAPTER SEVEN
Mastering the Vignette

This chapter explores the technique of using pivotal events to overlap threads among your characters in a way builds shared pasts and feels authentic to the reader. Working on multiple levels, you'll find and forge meaningful connections among characters and evolve backstories.

No matter which character you are writing—villain, hero or supporting character—getting to the heart of that character is essential. Readers want to look up to your hero, even when he is flawed. They want to hate—but understand—the motivations of your villain. And they want a supporting cast that draws them deeply in the story.

While I found literature that discussed the importance of this, I found no literature that explained how to accomplish it. The books I found focused on what I call the "macro" of writing characters. "Make your characters come alive" is wonderful advice, but what does it look like in practice, line by line, word by word? "Uncover your character's motivation" is another great bit of advice, but the author of the book only described what motivation was and why it was important in the novel. Writers want to know how to do it themselves. They want to see it in action and repeat it using their own ideas.

The hesitation that many writers feel as they push the words across the paper comes from not really knowing who their character. When you really know a character, the writing flows freely. You can describe them, explain what they're doing and envision what they will do at every turn. However, when you try to write characters before you've truly met them, it feels like playing "Connect the Dots" on a sheet of paper that's missing ¾ of the dots. The process is mentally exhausting and a monumental time waster.

Searching For A Solution

I searched for a solution that gets you (the writer) as close as possible to your character via the shortest and most direct path. More importantly, the writing you generate in this process is meaningful, essential and solidly written. For this section, I designed a system that guides you past the initial design phase of creating character and into deeper characterization.

I combed through books and online resources like "Write a letter to (or from) your character." The idea got me closer to explain the process, but the parameters of 'write a letter' were too broad and raised too many questions to lead to productive prose. It raised a flurry of questions. 'What kind of letter? From whom? About what?... and so on. I kept digging. The character maps that litter the internet were either too simple or so specific that a great deal of the content was irrelevant. While they were interesting to explore, the stop-and-go process felt forced and the writing didn't have the organic narrative flow that I needed. Another time-waster.

However, the two ideas did get me closer to a solution. I realized that visualization—seeing a character in action unrelated to the immediate story—provided a treasure trove of insight into the character. I picked up The Adventures of Tom Sawyer and read through the passage I remembered from years ago. Suddenly, the lightbulb came on. If you're familiar with the book by Mark Twain, you'll recall that Tom and Huck were no angels. In one scene, they walk in on their own funerals. This is the scene that I focus on to explain the importance of creating deep and resonant characters. I call this kind of writing a "vignette," a short, character sketch that depicts a specific scene or event. I use the concept of the 'eulogy' (macabre as the concept seems) because it sets the perfect parameters excavating the kind of information that you're looking for as you take this next step in character design.

Thinking Inside The Box

Rather than asking your brain to conjure up motivations and connections for a character from out of the blue, the eulogy technique narrows the focus of writing down to distinct, manageable and helpful parameters. It creates a box, if you will, that provides enough space for your creative mind to move without overwhelming it with useless information. Most of the pressure a writer feels when at the keyboard comes from tasking the brain to 'seek and find' answers in a sea of too much information. Essentially, you're asking your brain to function like a supercomputer; you're prompting your thinking mind to take the little bit you know of your character and create something entirely new without even knowing the boundaries of what you want to create. Is it any wonder that writers hit the brick wall we call 'writer's block'?

The technique of creating the vignettes asks your brain to scan a smaller information set. More importantly, it provides you a direct example by using parameters with clearly defined and familiar boundaries: the eulogy. This acts like a laser pointer for the reticular activating system (RAS) of the brain—that part of your brain responsible for seeking and locating information. The first time you do this, you'll find that it unleashes a flood of information. When your creative mind is unleashed inside a smaller space something amazing happens. Like a top wound tight before the release, the RAS goes wild and begins to locate cues and clues that are already in your narrative, buried in each character's unique story. Once unearthed, the effect is like a proverbial snowball, picking up every relevant detail and expanding the story as you gain momentum.

Before we begin that work, have a look at the scene I referenced from *The Adventures of Tom Sawyer.*

"Then there was a dispute about who saw the dead boys last in life, and many claimed that dismal distinction, and offered evidences, more or less tampered with by the witness; and when it was ultimately decided who DID see the departed last, and exchanged the last words with them, the lucky parties took upon themselves a sort of sacred importance, and

were gaped at and envied by all the rest. One poor chap, who had no other grandeur to offer, said with tolerably manifest pride in the remembrance:

"Well, Tom Sawyer he licked me once."

The villagers began to gather, loitering a moment in the vestibule to converse in whispers about the sad event... There was another communing silence, broken at intervals by muffled sobs, and then the minister spread his hands abroad and prayed. A moving hymn was sung, and the text followed: "I am the Resurrection and the Life."

As the service proceeded, the clergyman drew such pictures of the graces, the winning ways, and the rare promise of the lost lads that every soul there, thinking he recognized these pictures, felt a pang in remembering that he had persistently blinded himself to them always before, and had as persistently seen only faults and flaws in the poor boys. The minister related many a touching incident in the lives of the departed, too, which illustrated their sweet, generous natures, and the people could easily see, now, how noble and beautiful those episodes were, and remembered with grief that at the time they occurred they had seemed rank rascalities, well deserving of the cowhide. The congregation became more and more moved, as the pathetic tale went on, till at last the whole company broke down and joined the weeping mourners in a chorus of anguished sobs, the preacher himself giving way to his feelings, and crying in the pulpit.

There was a rustle in the gallery, which nobody noticed; a moment later the church door creaked; the minister raised his streaming eyes above his handkerchief, and stood transfixed! First one and then another pair of eyes followed the minister's, and then almost with one impulse the congregation rose and stared while the three dead boys came marching up the aisle, Tom in the lead, Joe next, and Huck, a ruin of drooping rags, sneaking sheepishly in the rear!"

Mark Twain. *The Adventures of Tom Sawyer*

How Authors Use The Vignette

Vignettes helps writers discover the links between characters and reveal shared past experiences of characters. Using the vignette, you'll create anecdotes to deepen your character's backstory and provide insight into character relationships and motivation. This technique gives your writing dimension and complexity. It allows you to pull back from the story and let the characters divulge information about one another in a way that feels authentic. It is a simple technique that produces wonderful results.

Tom & Huck provided the first example. The passage below can be found at the opening of "A Scandal in Bohemia." Here, Watson describes the character of Irene Adler, a woman whom Sherlock Holmes admires—due in part to the fact that she is one of the few people who have ever outwitted him. Watson reveals Sherlock's connection to Irene while simultaneously delineating Sherlock's eccentricities. As you read through, notice how closely this information resembles the kind of detail that emerges through vignettes.

Classic Fiction

> *"To Sherlock Holmes she is always the woman. I have seldom heard him mention her under any other name. In his eyes, she eclipses and predominates the whole of her sex. It was not that he felt any emotion akin to love for Irene Adler. All emotions, and that one particularly, were abhorrent to his cold, precise but admirably balanced mind. He was, I take it, the most perfect reasoning and observing machine that the world has seen, but as a lover he would have placed himself in a false position. He never spoke of the softer*

> *passions, save with a gibe and a sneer. They were admirable things for the observer—excellent for drawing the veil from men's motives and actions. But for the trained reasoner to admit such intrusions into his own delicate and finely adjusted temperament was to introduce a distracting factor which might throw a doubt upon all his mental results. Grit in a sensitive instrument, or a crack in one of his own high-power lenses, would not be more disturbing than a strong emotion in a nature such as his. And yet there was but one woman to him, and that woman was the late Irene Adler, of dubious and questionable memory."*
>
> Arthur Conan Doyle. *The Adventures of Sherlock Holmes*

- *Personality:* Watson makes it clear in this passage that Sherlock doesn't feel emotion, but defaults to intellect in order to assess the people around him.

- *Temperament:* Doyle does a fantastic job of sketching Sherlock's emotional, intellectual and interpersonal portrait as that intertwined triumvirate of weird, magnificent and ice cold that we've come to associate with every rendition of Sherlock.

- *Why It Works:* One of the reasons that this piece is so effective is because Watson uses Irene Adler as the vehicle for uncovering Sherlock's nature to the Reader. In one flowing description, Watson delves into Sherlock's emotions, connection to the opposite sex and his finely tuned intellect without overpowering the Reader with a list.

Building A Vignette

In this example, I placed Sio in the role of remembering Calendar. In doing so, I got great insight into the relationship of the two girls and also the entire group of flatmates. This technique created a more complex plot as well. Character eccentricities surfaced that led me down other paths with minor characters. Once I knew the boundaries of my characters, complicated and interesting opportunities for plot twists materialized.

FWM: Calendar's Vignette—Sio

" 'The first day I met Calendar, she taught me how to tie my shoelaces.' A ripple travelled through the church, but it was thin and abbreviated. The other side of it was heavy with pain. Every person seated in the church knew exactly what Sio was going through, and knew what it cost her to stand before them now.

'That August had been so hot that the air conditioner of the grammar school gave out. The teachers sent the entire school outside onto the playground. I found myself in a crush of children—all of them older, all of them strangers—and one of my shoelaces had come untied.'

Sio paused, reflecting back on that first day. She had hated school so far—all two hours of it—and she wanted to go home. She'd asked the teacher to call her mother after the first fifteen minutes and been met with a reproachful stare. Sio couldn't ask for her help again. Not for a shoelace.

So she'd sat down with her back against a tree and tried to remember how her mother had wound the laces into bunny ears. Her hair was sticking to the back of her neck and she was ready to cry.

Then Calendar appeared. She was skinny, smaller even than Sio, with a flaming red ponytail on the top of her head, skewing decidedly to the left.

' As I struggled with my shoelace and fought back tears, she sat down next to me with a look that day I'll never forget. Her first words to me were, 'Watch how I do this. I'm only going to do it once. So watch as if your life depends on it.'

'I'll confess, she scared me a little.''

More laughter, interspersed with nodding heads. Sio's eyes cut to Carter. A wry smile played at the corner of his mouth and she knew what he was thinking. 'If they only knew.'

She'd watched Calendar's eyes that day, her head bent over the laces, seen the pale blue of them dart to her own face then back again as Calendar crossed, turned and looped them into a perfect bow. The blue of Callie's eyes was the color of the ocean around an island. In many ways that's what Calendar was: an isolated, secret place that few—so very few had found.

'She showed me how to tie the shoe, undid the laces and said, "It's your turn. You can do this." And I did it on the first try. But that isn't what made us friends.'

Sio cleared her throat and looked down at the front pew. Ian's stony face was still and impassive, but he was passing Kleenex to Tomasz, who was fighting so hard to hold back the violent sobs that the pressure erupted in an enormous snot bubble. Talvert, sitting next to him didn't seem to notice. His handsome face had changed over the course of only a week, his sunken cheeks and hollow stare reminded her of someone who'd endured a long, grueling illness with the outcome still uncertain. Her eyes travelled to her husband's tear-soaked face, and she could see that he longed for the service to be over. Sio wanted this to be over so they could all go home and grieve in peace. But she owed this much to Calendar.

'After I tied my shoe, I asked Calendar if her mother could talk to my mother so she could come over and play.'

> *Sio shot a quick glance at Father Piu and saw the crease cut deeper at the corner of his eyes. She cleared her throat.*
>
> *'Without missing a beat, Cal told me that she was an orphan.'*
>
> *Sio stumbled over the word 'orphan.' She'd been so careful over the last twenty-three years to avoid it that the word felt treacherous in her mouth. She cleared her throat again.*
>
> *'She told me that she didn't have a mother who could call my mother. And it didn't really matter anyway because she'd already figured a way out of school and she wouldn't be there after lunch."*
>
> *Remembering the look on Calendar's face that day, Sio smiled.*
>
> *'That's when I knew that we were going to be best friends. Callie was my ticket home.'"*
>
> *Fiction Writing Maps: A Step-By-Step Guide To Characters*

Bits & Pieces

Though I obviously wouldn't use the entire vignette, the writing it generated provided me with parcels of information that I might easily insert into the novel.

For example, I can answer the question of how the characters met and expand on what I already have:

> *" 'How did you two meet?' Charles asked. Callie looked up from her soup and answered without missing a beat, 'We met in jail when we were eight years old.'*
>
> *Sio sputtered, trying to swallow the tomato bisque halfway down her throat.*
>
> *'You did not.' Charles countered, pinning Callie with a hard stare, but he knew that the more outlandish the statement from Callie, the more likely it was to be true.*

'Ask Judge Haglar if you don't believe me. He's the one who arrested us.' Callie scooped another spoonful of soup, shrugging off his look of disbelief.

Coughing with laughter, Sio explained. 'We met in school for Heaven's sake. Callie just said that to shock you. I met her the first day of first grade on the playground when the air conditioning went out.'

Charles face relaxed in relief, but he saw a swift look pass between the girls. His gaze rested on his wife—that sweet, cherubic face framed by Botticelli waves. She beamed angelically back at him.

'We'd already known each other for hours by the time we went to jail, Charles.'

Head bent over her soup, Callie's shoulders shook in silent laughter."

The Fiction Writing Maps: A Step-By-Step Guide To Characters

I can also use the writing from this vignette to let characters describe each other—a technique much more interesting than the overt description.

" 'What do you know of Callie's background? Where does she come from?" Charles asked. 'She's an or...an or...' Sio stumbled over the word. 'She's an orphan.'

Sio had been so careful over the last twenty-three years to avoid the word that it felt treacherous now in her mouth."

The Fiction Writing Maps: A Step-By-Step Guide To Characters

Planning The Vignette

This technique works best when you let the vignette play out visually before trying to capture it in print. As you "eulogize" each character that you're working on, take a step back and let the character present themselves rather than forcing preconceived notions on them. Though it's time-consuming, give each of the interconnected characters a chance to speak about the character you're working on. Focus on letting the connections bubble to the surface. Watch for the raw feelings on display. This provides a perfect opportunity to pinpoint where and how emotions manifest in your characters. Pay close attention so that you can use those telltale signs in your writing. Rather than having to dig for explanations of facial expressions such as 'a smile played at the corner of her mouth,' you may unearth non-verbal communications that you never considered before. When these appear organically from the vignettes, they feel more authentic to the characters.

The same holds true for noticing the expressions of other faces in the crowd. How do these characters show or hide their feelings, how do they respond to each other under pressure and how do they feel about being present at this emotional event? It's wise to have a notepad handy to jot your thoughts down as you complete each vignette. If you use the Livescribe 3 (see Writer's Resources), which I highly recommend, you can record your thoughts and have them show up as text on your desktop, saving time and effort in the process.

Mastering The Vignette

Below is a list of some places to begin as you create these character vignettes:

1. A brief chronological outline of the key events in this character's life.

2. Focus on pivotal events with key characters, such as how they met, first impressions, when they lost touch, etc.

3. Touch on a dominant event that rocked the character's life. Will it be lost in the dust of the past or will the repercussions echo? This allows you to explore grudges and future relationships.

4. Bring up small things that were important to the character. To who else did these things matter?

5. Highlight the character's good deeds, victories and struggles. What is their legacy? Who benefits from that legacy? This identifies alliances.

6. Where did the character feel that she failed? Is there someone to take up where she left off? This tells you who has a stake in your character's success and failure.

7. Focus on a character's less important activities. Though these may seem inconsequential, they provide the illusion of a real life layered with necessary and trivial activities. Who witnessed the inconsequential activities? This will tell you who your character's closest confidant was.

8. What have the other characters lost? A friend, a lover, an ally? Define those roles.

9. What critical plot points will not happen without this character? This helps you to define her stake in the story and helps generate plot twists.

CHAPTER EIGHT
Symbolism & Characterization

> Symbols are the cornerstone around which you build a strong character. In this chapter, you'll learn how to spotlight one personality trait for your character, deftly connect it to a meaningful symbol and weave that symbol throughout the novel.

If you think that finding a symbol for your character sounds too "literary" or complicated for the story that you're writing, bear in mind that many of the finest fictional characters have a signature symbol. And for a good reason. Symbols multitask in a story on an explicit and implicit level. By design, symbols are such and elemental and basic component of human communication that it would be a shame to leave this part out if you can possibly work it into your novel.

Consider that companies like Apple and Starbucks spend untold amounts of money to create and update their company symbols—or logos if you prefer. Over time, these symbols become the fundamental identification of a company and its products. All of the information of the company is unified into one distinct symbol. In many cases, Apple simply places the picture of the apple in many of its ads.

Symbols In Literature

Symbols in literature are like the swinging placards of the 15th century, those images that hung over storefronts to tell the townspeople where to find the baker and the blacksmith. Like those placards, symbols in literature let writers bypass a great deal of "telling" because they represent many layers of meaning. They provide explicit and implicit information about latent tendencies within each character.

Daenerys Targaryen's dragons and Harry Potter's lightning bolt scar are symbols, but they're also outward manifestations of the complex—and often competing—internal and external tension these characters feel. The dragon and the lightning bolt scar each have levels of violence and power associated with them. Symbols such as these might even forecast how characters will evolve on their character arcs.

Finding A Character's Symbol

A symbol does not have to be a physical item. Symbols can be as concrete as an animal, a medallion or a crucifix. They can be as abstract as emblem an idea, a memory or a poem. In order to activate the character's symbol, your readers need to understand it first. If you've chosen a well- known symbol, that won't take much work. But you can also create a new symbol by introducing a powerful story behind it that triggers emotion and forges a connection with the reader.

The character of Arya in George R. R. Martin's Game of Thrones series owned a sword called "Needle." This sword was her symbol. It represented who she was, who she wasn't and who she hoped to become. We might say that it symbolized her core values. This is precisely what a symbol is meant to do in a novel.

A great tool for finding your character's symbol is *The Book of Symbols: Reflections on Archetypal Images.* This compendium of symbols explores everything from the plant world to the cosmos and all points in between. It provides an overview of each well-known symbol and gives examples from Art, History, Nature and Religion that are expertly researched and beautifully presented.

You might also explore actual artifacts to find your character's symbol. If your story is set in a time period that is easily accessible, spend some time scanning paintings, ephemera and sculpture of the era. These are replete with fabulous images and tableaus that tell their own stories. When you find one that you like, copy it and save it to Scrivener. Use it as the icon for your character and go deeper into its possible meanings. Explore the nuances of color, texture, psychological and temporal meaning that this symbol might have for your character. In this way, can build layer upon layer of meaning and connection between characters and their symbols. This builds engagement and empowers your readers to look more deeply into the text.

Historical References

Historical references and coats of arms are also a fabulous place to find symbols. Searching online archives can be time-consuming, but you can always narrow your search down to an era or a specific landmark and streamline the process with an image search. Even if your setting is entirely fictitious, your symbol can still be real. George R. R. Martin used the wolf, the sigils and even architectural features like The Wall as unifying symbols in his novels. The possibilities are—without exaggeration—endless.

Once you settle on a symbol, consider how you'll use it in your story. Where will you introduce it? How will you make it relevant to the character? Once introduced, how will you keep that symbol in play? Will the symbol change as the character changes or will the character evolve to fit the symbol? These are all good questions to consider as you firm up your decision.

An effective way to build out your symbol is to work inside of Scrivener. The software allows you to pull in web pages, images and create notes on the symbol. The Fiction Writing Map Template designed for Scrivener has a specific place where you can work on your symbol alongside great examples from literature. We've also added a fabulous link where you can explore your character's symbol in a web pattern that encompasses everything from body language to character action and observations.

Symbolism In Literature

E. M Forster, the author of *A Room with a View*, is widely regarded as one of the best writers of his generation. The characters he created are compelling, the descriptions magnificent. The journey of Lucy Honeychurch from youthful, naïve Italian tourist to independent, fully-formed version of womanhood is exquisitely devised.

For those who haven't seen the movie, it is an easy-to-follow and truly epic film. Daniel Day Lewis will never be as consummately geeky as when he portrayed Cecil Vyse. Helena Bonham Carter catapulted to fame with her role as Lucy Honeychurch. Together they make *A Room With a View* a poignant and beautiful film.

The character of Cecil Vyse gives us one of the most straightforward examples of how a character's symbol intersects with plot, theme and setting. I will use examples from this novel more than once throughout the book because Forster's writing is technically marvelous.

Here's how Forster introduces Cecil in the text *just prior* to the quote below: "Appearing thus late in the story, Cecil must be at once be described." (E. M. Forster. *A Room with a View*). *That's it.* That is all the reader gets before Cecil steps onto the stage in the next paragraph. So, if you ever tear your hair out worrying about your character introduction, go back and reread that sentence. Take a deep breath and realize that you can keep it simple and still be brilliant.

Classic Fiction

> *"He was medieval. Like a Gothic statue. Tall and refined, with shoulders that seemed braced square by an effort of the will, and a head that was tilted a little higher than the usual level of vision, he resembled those fastidious saints who guard the portals of a French cathedral. Well educated, well endowed, and not deficient physically, he remained in the grip of a certain devil whom the modern world knows as self-consciousness, and whom the medieval, with dimmer vision, worshipped as asceticism."*
>
> E. M. Forster. *A Room with a View*

- *Symbol:* Notice how Forster doesn't say Cecil "looked Medieval," but the he "**was** Medieval...like a Gothic statue." This is deliberate and perfect choice of words. Poor Cecil isn't pretending. He's made of stone on the inside and literally defined by his antiquated idealization of womanhood and social structures. The next sentence is both a sentence fragment and a simile. This syntax fairly screams "pay attention to what I'm saying about the character here." This is something more than beautiful prose; *it's dastardly effective prose.* Not only does it sum up Cecil perfectly, but it reflects a central theme in the novel: the stringent Edwardian society that surrounds Lucy, and one from which she finally escapes, is embodied by the man she nearly marries. She was that close to catastrophe.

- *Why It Works:* Simple and brilliant, this is precisely how you use a short descriptive passage to introduce a symbol. The words are chosen with great care. They evoke images and archetypes. Not one detail, not one adjective in this paragraph, goes unused by Forster later in the novel. As the relationship between Cecil and Lucy evolves, Cecil's haughtiness and cool interior manifest in action within the plot. His actions and her responses create conflict and reinforce his symbol in a perfect, circular motion.

- *Possibilities:* The most important take-away from this passage is this—the symbol that you attribute to a character adds another layer of meaning to character relationships and the plot itself. This doesn't have to be epic. It can be incredibly simple. It can be the oversized and overpriced stroller from London that your character just had to have. "It made life miserable twenty-three hours out of the day. She and Charles bumped past it coming and going. Her little toe was perpetually blue from the times that she'd caught it on the wheel as she stumbled to Charlotte's room in a half-blind haze of fatigue. But that one hour out of the day—the walk—made it all worth it. The blue and chrome confection of British luxury fairly preened along the path of Central Park and drew the eyes of all the other young mothers. Strolling behind it, Caroline felt brilliant. Grand. Something more than ordinary." The stroller is simply a vehicle—a symbol—that helps the reader understand more about the character.

- *Note:* Remember to keep tying your symbol back to theme, plot and character. Blend it in again and again as if you were working brushstrokes of color with each pass of your text over the symbol itself.

What Does My Character Resemble?

Symbols not only give characters depth, but also give readers a great deal of implicit information. In *The Hobbit*, Tolkien uses a blind fish as a symbol to help readers connect to an impression for Gollum. He never *explicitly* compares Gollum to a fish, but presents it through metaphor and continues to weave that description into his narrative about Gollum. Gollum's pale eyes, the slimy island he lives on, the way he moves without making a ripple all contribute to building this symbolism.

Because his character was entirely fictitious, Tolkien had to use a common image that would help readers visualize Gollum. The comparison to a pale-eyed, slimy fish gave readers information they could import to create a representation of Gollum. As gruesome as he is, Gollum has become one of the most well-known characters in literature because Tolkien drafted him with such painstaking clarity.

To find Gollum's symbol, Tolkien obviously gave some thought to what might happen to a creature who lived in perpetual darkness, away from the company of people. He also dug into Gollum's backstory to list the few key character flaws that set him on the course to living in his dismal, underground pool. When you begin by making this list for your character, you not only find a symbol, but you achieve coherence in characterization that resonates with readers.

To find an accurate comparison for your character, begin making a list of their outward characteristics. When you have enough to work with, Quick Write anything and everything you can think of that pertains to that characteristic. I'm including my messy, unedited first version so that you can see how work in progress really looks as you wander through symbolism.

Callie's Outward Characteristics

1. Petite

2. Blue Eyes

3. Calculating Intelligence

4. Independent

Then, I'll take up on each of those keywords and "discuss" with myself what that really looks like in the novel and why it's important to my character's development (if it actually is).

Quick Write

1. Petite: Calendar stands 5'5 ½"

> "In a world of investigators, men who made their living by the size of their biceps rather than their brains, Calendar had learned to use her size to advantage. Her small frame put people at ease, made them believe they had nothing to fear from her. But nothing could be further from the truth."
>
> *What does this remind me of?*

2. Blue eyes:

"Talvert had seen that color blue once before snorkeling off the coast of Caneel Bay as the dying sun hit the water in one last blaze before sunset. Cal's eyes were the same shade, a deepy, crystalline that drew you down and down. And deeper still.

He'd kept her talking to see if he could discover the hint of a contact lens at the outer edge that would tell him the truth of it—that eyes that color didn't exist in nature.

He had thought he was watching her, asking her questions in quick succession to force her to concentrate onto his face. It was only when the conversation slowed for a minute and she continued to stare back at him, boldly and without blinking, that he realized the truth. Like a diver surfacing, he sucked in deep breath and blinked to get his bearings. The blue was a siren's song. How far from shore had he gone? How long he had been staring?

Long enough, he knew, to be in over his head."

3. Calculating intelligence:

"Calendar couldn't be easily explained. To say that she was 'smart' missed the mark. She was stone cold, focused calculation. She was decisive and radical in her investigative approach, and so cleverly nuanced that she made even the most seasoned investigators look like fumbling fools. By the time they'd figured out her strategy, it was always too late."

4. Independent:

> *"There's something about being an orphan that changes you. The moment you realize you're truly alone in the world—without a mother or father—you feel a snap as if a giant, cosmic rubber band yanked you irrevocably to the other side of a chasm that separates you from 'the rest of the world.'*
>
> *Some strange Darwinian switch goes off in that moment. From then on, your guard is always up, you're cautious of the world around you, distrustful of strangers and forever— unrelentingly—alone."*

After going through this exercise, I referred back to *The Book of Symbols* and flipped quickly through until I landed on the one symbol that I could connect—both through significance in the story and to the character herself. Once I found that symbol, I began making a web for it. With the symbol in the middle, I branched into anything and everything that connected back to that symbol and to my character. I went beyond words and text and added everything that came to mind: colors, textures, smells and memories. I tried to pull in as many of the senses as I could to build out the symbol.

Here, I've given an example of Talvert's symbol.

FWM: Talvert

> *"Women who knew him described him as a Renaissance Man: rattling off a list of his past accomplishments that ranged from four registered patents to a bronze sculpture made by his own hands that was on permanent display at the local 'Guns & Wellies' shop on Main Street.*

> *Men called him a 'man's man' and left it at that—the two all-encompassing words of virility and expertise having done their work. Anyone might have assumed the descriptions were overblown. Until they met Talvert. Then they realized that he was both—and probably much more.*
>
> *From head to toe, Talvert was built as if he'd been cast from a mold of the masters of the Renaissance. He stood six-foot two—not so tall that he towered, but tall enough to handle anything that came his way. His features, too, were chiseled in the understated perfection of the Florentines: strong chin, classic nose, arms and thighs that looked like skin pulled taught over stone. Add to that a perfect education and a scathingly sharp wit, and it was clear to everyone why he was still unmarried at thirty-two. 'Being Talvert's wife would make any woman feel inadequate' one of the ladies in the God Squad said over breakfast at the bistro. That was the truth of it. So far no woman had the courage to even try."*
>
> *The Fiction Writing Maps: A Step-By-Step Guide To Characters*

- *Figurative Language:* I didn't feel comfortable with any simile or metaphor to describe Talvert so I substituted a phrase that served both the purpose of the story structure and the purpose of depiction better.

- *Comparison:* I used the two comparisons because they both fit the portrait I've drafted of Talvert. His personality will cover that entire landscape—from the physical and masculine activities to the more cerebral and eccentric hobbies I've given him.

- *Why It Works:* It reads a bit overblown, and I haven't quite found the voice I'm looking, but I've gotten one step closer to figuring out who Talvert is. More importantly, everything that I've added in this passage has implications within the story structure.

- *What Didn't Work Well:* The words "Renaissance Man" aren't really evocative enough to provide a clear visual. I might go back and dig around for a more precise word to use as my "symbol" for Talvert.

- *Possibilities:* I haven't met the person yet who could come close to Cecil Vyse, but I hope that studying Forster's example helped me create a character whose traits intersected well with the theme and the plot details.

Aside: I took the description of Talvert from a group of Florentine Carabinieri (police) walking ahead of me on the Ponte Vecchio in Florence. Such figures do exist. Travelling is truly inspirational.

Examples In Fiction

Symbols don't have to be hidden or too "literary." They can be overt. They can even be outward characteristics as in *Anne of Green Gables*. Like Harry Potter's scar, Anne's hair sets her apart. This outward symbol helps frame the character and drives much of the action and dialogue as Anne gets into one scrape after another because of the personality traits and the "burden" associated with having red hair.

Even a symbol like Sherlock's violin tells the reader something more about the character. Presumably, Doyle chose the violin in order to highlight Sherlock's personality that values precision and mastery. Had Sherlock had played ping pong rather than violin, he would have been a far different character.

Explore the example I pulled from *Anne of Green Gables*. See if you can pinpoint how the symbolism used helps define the character.

Classic Fiction

> *"Yes, it's red," she said resignedly. "Now you see why I can't be perfectly happy. Nobody could who has red hair. I don't mind the other things so much— the freckles and the green eyes and my skinniness. I can imagine them away. I can imagine that I have a beautiful rose-leaf complexion and lovely starry violet eyes. But I cannot imagine that red hair away. I do my best. I think to myself, 'Now my hair is a glorious black, black as the raven's wing.' But all the time I know it is just plain red and it breaks my heart. It will be my lifelong sorrow. I read of a girl once in a novel who had a lifelong sorrow but it wasn't red hair. Her hair was pure gold rippling back from her alabaster brow. What is an alabaster brow? I never could find out. Can you tell me?"*
>
> L. M. Montgomery. *Anne of Green Gables*

- *Symbol:* The symbol associated with Anne is her red hair and freckles. The word "red" is repeated five times in that one paragraph—six, if you count the homophone "read." This repetition alerts a young reader to the importance of that point.

- *Why It Works:* Red hair is associated with specific character traits that Montgomery puts into play throughout the novel. Anne starts off as a spindly, unattractive girl with a vivid imagination and a hot temper. All of the subsequent foibles and upsets stem in one way or another from her hair color and the traits associated with it.

The Enchanted April by Elizabeth Von Arnim features the fabulous character, Lady Caroline Dester, the perfect female embodiment of entitled dissatisfaction to appear anywhere in literature. Lady Caroline, a stunning London socialite, retreats to Portofino with an unlikely group to escape the burden of London's society and contemplate the shallow emptiness of her life following the death of a man she loved.

In this novel, Von Arnim paints Lady Caroline as a jaded socialite struggling through what can only be described as a bitter ennui—boredom, to the rest of us. It is that boredom that becomes her symbol.

Though "dissatisfaction" isn't tangible, it's a mood marker that indicates the larger idea behind Lady Caroline's personal struggle. Just as red hair is associated with certain personality traits, Lady Caroline's status and discontent are associated with the elite snobbery of a debutante. It infuses every thought, word and action. This works incredibly well as a device for this character. Lady Caroline is the only person alive who could feel discontent while on a holiday in Portofino. The absurdity of that point only heightens the use of the device within the novel as you can see in the next example.

Classic Fiction

> *"If they had got out of their shells so immediately, at the very first contact, unless she checked them they would soon begin to press upon her, and then good-bye to her dream of thirty restful, silent days, lying unmolested in the sun, getting her feathers smooth again, not being spoken to, not waited on, not grabbed at and monopolized, but just recovering from the fatigue, the deep and melancholy fatigue, of the too much."*
>
> **Elizabeth Von Arnim.** *The Enchanted April*

- *Symbol:* The symbol associated with Lady Caroline is discontent. Though Lady Caroline appears to have everything—youth, beauty, privilege and title— she is unhappy and sick of the London social life and its emptiness.

- *Language:* Von Arnim uses evocative language that helps to characterize Lady Caroline. The word choice reinforces her discontent: "silent, not being spoken to, not grabbed at, unmolested" are only a few in the long string of words that help typify Lady Caroline. Von Arnim ends this paragraph with the final fabulous four words—Lady Caroline has come to Italy to recover from a life of the "of the too much."

- *Why It Works:* This symbol works not only on its own as a defining feature of Lady Caroline, but also as a thread that weaves into the story and affects Lady Caroline's actions, her thoughts and the thoughts and responses of other characters.

Final Thoughts On Symbols

As you choose your character's symbol, leave every possibility open. Remember that it doesn't have to be a classic symbol; it just needs to be appropriate to the character. That said, a symbol should work on multiple levels and should bring something more with it than just an image. Think back to Katniss Everdeen and the Mockingjay. That symbol evolved. It originated as the hybrid bird—the Mockingjay. Throughout the novel, the reader see Katniss take on the traits of the bird and them evolve those even further until the symbol comes to represent the bravery of Katniss herself. It is precisely this kind of symbolism that readers adore. They want to open not one book, but a book with layer upon layer that they can dig into and dissect. Choose a symbol that suits that purpose and you'll delight your readers.

Symbolism & Characterization

Step 1: What one item or idea emerges organically from the situation surrounding your character? What two or three specific character traits can you point to as clear, commonly-understood visuals that would show that? Write those out now in complete, unedited thoughts

_____

_____

_____

_____

Step 2: What comparison can you use that is unrelated to those traits, but matches exactly? Think of two or more words or descriptions that support or elaborate on that trait. (They needn't be physical. They can be architectural, structural, cultural or historical.) Write those out now in complete, unedited thoughts

_____

_____

_____

_____

Step 3: How does the first item or symbol translate to your character's upbringing, education, mental or emotional landscape? How does the symbol describe what your character is not? Write those out now in complete, unedited thoughts

_____

_____

_____

_____

_____

_____

Step 4: Where else in the novel can you integrate that symbol? Does it connect directly or indirectly to another character, plot point or event? Write those out now in complete, unedited thoughts

_____

_____

_____

_____

_____

_____

CHAPTER NINE
Heroic Traits

In this section, we'll uncover the "ordinary extraordinary" in your main characters. The most intriguing and gratifying characters don't broadcast their laudable traits, but insist that the readers chisel around them and pry them loose during the course of the story.

Each bestselling literary hero began as a small player in a larger game. Bilbo Baggins, Katniss Everdeen and Scarlett O'Hara were virtual unknowns on Page 1 of their respective novels. By the end of each book, each had risen to greatness in their fictitious world. The characters we hail as great literary heroes are often not that different from ourselves. In fact, some of the most compelling heroes, like Oliver Twist or Bilbo Baggins, might be categorized as absolutely ordinary, but for a few features that separate them from the rest of humanity.

A hero might begin as a common Hobbit in the Shire, but he must eventually prove that he deserves to become a central player in the epic game. His success or failure, his life or death will determine the future in this fictitious world. This is how common characters become great heroes. Readers of fiction want to aspire to those heights, to live a life so deeply meaningful, so epic that their success resonates far and wide. This is why we love heroes.

The Five Key Traits of Heroes

I compared countless novels to locate the identical traits of characters like Frodo Baggins and Katniss Everdeen. Though these characters are of different age groups and genders, I found that heroes share five critical traits that I've isolated to help write larger-than-life characters:

- They Command Respect From Peers
- They Convert "Difficult" To "Simple"
- Their Life Has Overarching Meaning
- They Exhibit A Flawed Human Nature
- They Flex Their Willpower

The Ordinary Extraordinary

In the next section, I'll show you and how to uncover the "ordinary extraordinary" in your characters. As you do this work, keep the "less is more" approach in mind. The most intriguing and gratifying characters don't broadcast their laudable traits. They often don't even know they possess any heroic traits (the readers might not know either) until the story is nearly over. Ineptitude, absurdity and incongruousness are more often the hallmarks of great heroes than wisdom, skill and noble birth. Keep an eye out for that moment in your story when you can highlight the unassuming or unpretentious and make it astonishing. And remember that it isn't just the main character who deserves distinction. It's acceptable to build some of these heroic traits into your supporting cast as well—but to a lesser degree.

By way of quick example, Sam Gamgee in *Lord of the Rings* exhibited all the traits listed in this chapter though he is not technically the protagonist of the novel. Moreover, he held firm when the moment called for it, toiled the long road with Frodo and suffered without much irritation or complaint. He was a heroic minor character, in keeping with his role as a sidekick.

Command Respect From Peers

Reader respect is earned as we see a character navigate through trouble, making bad decisions, altering her course, and amending her thoughts and actions to achieve a true aim towards the end result—whatever that outcome might be.

People who exert control over difficult situations command respect. Landmark characters act and react in a way that earns them respect from other characters—and often from the villain. Because humans are social animals, we admire and follow other with strong leadership skills. When readers see other characters defer to leadership, they feel that deference. When a character wins a leadership role in the novel, your reader echoes the respect that the other characters feel. This is how heroic literary figures become national (and global) icons.

How do you build a hero that commands respect? You set him up to fail. Epically. The seeds of respect are sown in multiple, gut-wrenching defeats. Set your character up to fail, then let him claw his way out of the well of despair, bloodied and determined to succeed next time. Failure and the response to failure is a critical aspect of creating resonant characters.

Classic Fiction

"Through the night armed men had been coming stealthily, silently, from all sides; and in the early morning, before dawn, his flanking parties were attacked. unaggressive, so good-humoured, so simple, that none could resist it; ribaldry and blasphemy were instinctively hushed in his presence, and even the most hardened ruffian was softened by his contact. But a couple of years before he would naturally have been put on half-pay under the age limit, a little expedition was arranged against some unruly hill-tribes, and Colonel Parsons was given the command. He took the enemy by surprise, finding them at the foot of the hills, and cut off, by means of flanking bodies, their retreat through the two passes behind. He placed his guns on a line of hillocks to the right, and held the tribesmen in the hollow of his hand. He could have massacred them all, but nothing was farther from his thoughts. He summoned them to surrender, and towards evening the headmen came in and agreed to give up their rifles next day; the night was cold, and dark, and stormy. The good Colonel was delighted with the success both of his stratagem and of his humanity. He had not shed a single drop of blood."

W. Somerset Maugham. *The Hero.*

Convert "Difficult" To "Simple"

Anyone who has ever fought their way through a group project knows that the one who emerges as the leader is the one who unravels the knot of the problem and lays the path forward out in a straight line for others to follow. Readers crave empowerment.

As you fling problems at your characters, they should eventually become better at overcoming obstacles. This also is a common trait of great literary heroes. Throughout the course of the novel, your character begins to "get it".... whatever "it" is within the context of your story. Ultimately, your character not only overcomes obstacles more easily, but also starts to convert these problems into solutions. That turning point is where your character rounds the corner to greatness.

Katniss Everdeen in The Hunger Games is a good example to illustrate this dynamic. Over the course of the novel, her ability to discern danger and find solutions evolves as she's subjected to one trial after another. This marks the ascension of the hero to legendary status. By the end of the novel, Katniss has not only overcome all the obstacles, but turned the tables and created an obstacle for the other side. What occurs within the character arc of heroes is a Darwinian evolution of the character. They are either the one who leads or the last one left standing.

Some characters are presented as "gifted" in one area or another. They have an uncanny ability that sets the apart from others. Read through any Sherlock Holmes and you'll see that Doyle makes certain to underscore Sherlock's genius. However, Doyle also saddles Sherlock with a handicap as you'll see in the next excerpt.

Classic Fiction

> *"I could not help laughing at the ease with which he explained his process of deduction.*
> *"When I hear you give your reasons," I remarked, "the thing always appears to me to be*
> *so ridiculously simple that I could easily do it myself, though at each successive instance of*
> *your reasoning I am baffled until you explain your process. And yet I believe that my eyes*
> *are as good as yours."*
>
> Arthur Conan Doyle. *The Adventures of Sherlock Holmes.*

Frail Human Nature

> *This list of attributes begins with the first, most basic, attribute: a very human nature.*
> *Characters who resonate as heroic show us both the best and the worst in themselves.*
> *Showing your character's unattractive side within the context of the novel is absolutely*
> *necessary.*

Your readers are human. They have thoughts and failings that they prefer not to show. Most of the time, our conscious, more compassionate mind stifles that ugliness. However, reader need to see your characters in their totality—warts and all. Only then can you reveal your character's compassionate, social self. Showing this interplay of conflicting emotions to the reader makes your character seem more lifelike, more approachable. This becomes critically important if your character exhibits phenomenal skills in other areas. No one wants to read about a character who is so far evolved that they have no flaws, no foibles and they take on the world with wild success in five chapters. That's not only unrealistic; it's boring.

Readers want to see imperfect characters who struggle, and they love characters as much for their ability to combat their failings as for their achievements. A character who fights against her worst impulses not only seems real, but generates compassion and empathy in the reader. It is those failings that give readers hope. When they see a fictional character overcoming fear, it teaches them the way to courage.

As you begin to build your character's personality, search the archetype list for examples of less attractive traits that might fit your character. However, be careful not to go too far. Don't make your character out to be a bully and Do show your character recognizing his own failings and struggling to distance himself from those failings. That kind of self-knowledge and willpower define the hero.

Classic Fiction

> *"My own complete happiness, and the home-centred interests which rise up around the man who first finds himself master of his own establishment, were sufficient to absorb all my attention, while Holmes, who loathed every form of society with his whole Bohemian soul, remained in our lodgings in Baker Street, buried among his old books, and alternating from week to week between ITCaine and ambition, the drowsiness of the drug, and the fierce energy of his own keen nature."*
>
> Arthur Conan Doyle. *The Adventures of Sherlock Holmes*

Willpower

> *Willpower isn't something that your character "has." It's an asset that is built through challenge, choice and exertion until he "owns" it.*

Willpower is the road salt sprinkled on the icy driveway of our everyday lives. It helps us gain traction to move out of whatever rut we find ourselves in and hit the open road to greatness. It is that resolve that readers adore. At their core, readers yearn for strength of will because they know it's worth.

Characters who resonate with readers don't sit idly by and allow things to simply happen. They take control of the situation. No matter how exhausted they are, no matter what wounds they suffered and no matter how poor the odds of success may seem, they drag themselves up and find ways to leverage control over uncontrollable situations. They slog. They groan. They grapple. They might not succeed in every instance, but fortune favors them because they find the will to try.

Make your character's road slippery in places. Let your readers see him slide, right himself or go down. Then scatter road salt in places to help him gain traction. But do it in a believable way. If you can make your reader feel the suffering as your character wobbles to hold his footing, they'll enjoy the triumph that much more.

The best fictional example of willpower I could find was in Jane Eyre. After leaving Thornfield Hall, Jane endures a long, lonely stretch without friend or home. In fact, she very nearly dies in this part of the novel. She could easily have given in and gone back to comfort and a man who loved her, but her desire to live an authentic, autonomous life spurred her on:

Classic Fiction

"But I was a human being, and had a human being's wants: I must not linger where there was nothing to supply them. I rose; I looked back at the bed I had left. Hopeless of the future, I wished but this—that my Maker had that night thought good to require my soul of me while I slept; and that this weary frame, absolved by death from further conflict with fate, had now but to decay quietly, and mingle in peace with the soil of this wilderness. Life, however, was yet in my possession, with all its requirements, and pains, and responsibilities. The burden must be carried; the want provided for; the suffering endured; the responsibility fulfilled. I set out.

Whitcross regained, I followed a road which led from the sun, now fervent and high. By no other circumstance had I will to decide my choice. I walked a long time, and when I thought I had nearly done enough, and might conscientiously yield to the fatigue that almost overpowered me—might relax this forced action, and, sitting down on a stone I saw near, submit resistlessly to the apathy that clogged heart and limb."

Charlotte Brontë. *"Jane Eyre: An Autobiography."*

Finding The Perfect Flaw

> *Character flaws are built from the scars of past wounds. The best ones are parsed out as the novel progresses—given in small chunks that align perfectly with the tension and the moment of the story.*

Well-rounded characters—like real people—have personalities that include unlikeable and even negative characteristics. If you've created a character with no negative traits, your hero is already sunk. Just as every villain has at least one redeeming quality, every Pollyanna has a wart.

The simple truth is that flawless characters are dull. Their shiny exterior has no bumps, no frayed fabric and no shortcomings to make them interesting. While readers want protagonists who metaphorically and literally kick ass, they also long for user-friendly heroes in whom they recognize themselves. Those tiny - or not so tiny—rips and tears in the costumes of fictional characters leave behind straggling threads of imperfection that allow your readers to "tie into" your character. The hero's flaw makes him relatable - it's the dented bumper on a Porsche that puts heroism inside the reach of regular mortals. Readers believe in the fictional character you've created because they can point to that same flaw in themselves. By extrapolation, they secretly believe themselves capable of the heroism your character exhibits because of the common flaw they share.

Who doesn't want to be a brilliant criminalist, an aerospace engineer for NASA or a small-town forensic scientist who saves a small town from a serial killer?

However, to make the extraordinary attributes of your hero seem more realistic, you have to hobble a hero with at least one relatable flaw.

The perfect flaw will connect back to thoughts and actions that vibrate with strong feelings and emotions. Most successful character flaws stem from past wounds. These wounds have their origin in past events that left a character with pain, shame or blame. Backstory is the vehicle that carries that information.

Characters are tricky beasts. They'll develop quirks and eccentricities to avoid facing their pasts and the pain that comes with it. Sherlock Holmes staunched his pain in drugs. A definite flaw. Bilbo Baggins succumbed, in part, to the power of the Ring. Another flaw, which fortunately did not affect him as powerfully as it did Gollum. Gollum was lost to greed.

The flaw itself does not have to be grievous. Greed, for example, isn't at the top of the scale as flaws go. The heroic aspect of character lies in the struggle—not the wound. We saw this in Frodo Baggins as he fought to keep from putting the Ring on his finger. The "perfect flaw" for a character highlights the pain of the struggle and builds the tension. The tension mandates a need for the character to exert willpower to become a hero.

In this first example, we see one of the most famous flaws in literature. Pride and Prejudice illustrates how a character's fatal flaw can serve as the overarching theme of a novel. Here, we see Mr. Darcy reject Elizabeth Bennett as a dancing partner because of her looks. It's interesting to note that Austen explores every argument on this theme, from prejudice as a form of protection against the greedy grasping of the social climbers to its harshest and most callous forms.

Classic Fiction

> "She is tolerable, but not handsome enough to tempt me; I am in no humour at present to give consequence to young ladies who are slighted by other men. You had better return to your partner and enjoy her smiles, for you are wasting your time with me."
>
> Jane Austen. *Pride and Prejudice*

Characters such as Darcy rarely see the totality of their flaws. It makes them endearing, frustrating, charming and human. While characters get a glimpse of the unappealing parts of their make up throughout the course of a novel, the reader sees their faults in full.

Here is Doyle again to illustrate how you might use another character to frame your hero's flaw.

Classic Fiction

> "But consider!" I said, earnestly. "Count the cost! Your brain may, as you say, be roused and excited, but it is a pathological and morbid process, which involves increased tissue-change and may at last leave a permanent weakness. You know, too, what a black reaction comes upon you. Surely the game is hardly worth the candle. Why should you, for a mere passing pleasure, risk the loss of those great powers with which you have been endowed? Remember that I speak not only as one comrade to another, but as a medical man to one for whose constitution he is to some extent answerable."
>
> Arthur Conan Doyle. *The Adventures of Sherlock Holmes.*

Heroic Traits

Step 1: Think of the ways that your character might command respect from his peer group? This might be through brawn, brains, experience or his place in the social hierarchy. Write those out now in complete, unedited thoughts

_____

_____

_____

_____

_____

Step 2: What can your character do that is easy for him, but difficult for others? Can you think of a time in your novel when everything is about to fall apart, but the character simplifies the problem by using this ability? Write those out now in complete, unedited thoughts

_____

_____

_____

_____

Step 3: How can you connect your character to a greater purpose? Is there a way to drive your character even deeper into that purpose through a tragedy, chance encounter or plot point? Write those out now in complete, unedited thoughts

_____

_____

_____

_____

_____

Step 4: To help your character flex his willpower, look for that one place that he dares not go. It doesn't need to be huge or terrifying to everyone—but it needs to be a monumental effort for him. Let him skirt around it, walk away and suffer. Then lead him back again for the final push. Write those out now in complete, unedited thoughts

_____

_____

_____

_____

_____

_____

Step 5: To find your character's flaw, look at what his greatest strength is—then move in the opposite direction. Characters who are driven to do great things are often running from demons of past failures. What fear or failure is hiding behind your character's strengths? Write those out now in complete, unedited thoughts

_____

_____

_____

_____

_____

_____

CHAPTER TEN

The Writing Compass

> *Here, I explain how to write a brief opening scene using the writing that you've already generated. I discuss how to create a Narrative, anchor characters in the Setting, parse Exposition, and finally Weave in action, thoughts, observation, responses and dialogue to create a simple, solid scene.*

Before you begin, open any great book you have on the shelf and read through an entire scene. I'll wait ☺

Writers have refined the technique of writing the novel. They've agreed on certain, simple parameters for conveying story. And readers have come to appreciate and expect novels that follow this familiar design. When you nail this technique, it leads to polished and industry standard prose.

After reading through and annotating hundreds of passages in countless books, I discovered the commonalities of the basic scene. Scenes are made of distinct parts:

narrative, character thoughts and observations, action, character responses and dialogue. I drafted that list and studied these elements side-by-side in scene after scene so I could explain how you'll work them into your own writing.

Like real people, characters think, feel, observe, act and respond. Though every writer approaches it differently, all of those elements are included in a well-written scene. At times, you might have larger sections of narrative or long stretches of dialogue. However, a scene with no character thought feels 'off' to the reader. A scene with little or no action feels stagnant. Complete the entire circuit—narrative, thought, observation, action, responses and dialogue—to achieve a balanced scene that gives the reader a satisfying sense of completion.

As I pointed out at the beginning of the book, crafting the perfect scene belongs in another writing resource all its own. *The Fiction Writing Maps: Charting the Scenic Route* is already near completion and will explore scene writing in depth.

But I understand that you want to flex your character writing muscles now! Be sure to visit The Fiction Writing Maps for more on this topic as well as threaded discussions from writers in progress.

Crafting The Scene

One thing you might have noticed is that the action in the scene does not take place in precise, chronological order. Most, if not all, scenes are broken up into chunks. You probably read through a scene with at least one character speaking, engaging in action, thinking about the past, planning his next move, responding to another character or event in the setting, then explaining some significant detail about the plot. These are explicit packets of information woven together, piece by piece, to create the scene.

Crafting the scene can be the hardest part in getting the novel rolling. As I pointed out in the section on vignettes, when you begin something new—like a scene—you begin with what appears to be a blank slate. However, nothing could be further from the truth. The white page only seems empty. Within that white lies every color imagined and every word, phrase, paragraph and novel every written.

You're asking your brain to pull one perfect word from an ether of infinity just to begin. What we call writer's block is nothing more than the circuit overload that happens when your writing parameters are too wide. The Writing Compass helps to narrow those parameters. North, South, East and West provide the compass points to for everything you need in a scene, and they are broken down like this:

North: The straightforward narrative. Here is where you tell the reader distinctly what has happened, what is happening and what will happen. It's the nuts and bolts of the story.

South: Significant action within a setting. In each scene, there is at least one significant action upon which the scene turns. Without it, there is no scene. This is the pivot point to which the action flows and from which it moves in another direction. The setting provides the boundaries as a stage for the action.

East: Explanation and Exposition. As the action moves forward, you must parse out explanation and exposition in order to keep the momentum moving forward.

West: Weave in connecting material. Between Narrative, Action, Explanation and Exposition are the spaces where you weave the elements of thought, observation, response, dialogue and description to complete the writing circuit.

The Basic Scene Template

Scene:

Narrative: *Discuss explicitly what is happening at the beginning moment of the scene.*

Exposition: *Provide the reader any parcel of information they need in order to understand the present moment.*

Significant Action: *Explain in simple detail the significant action of the character or characters.*

Weave: *Add dialogue, thought, observation or response: tie these all back in again to the narrative and exposition.*

This scene template represents the most simplistic format, but it is a quick and easy way to map out a scene. It encompasses all four points in the Writing Compass. Again, this is just a starting point. It provides smaller parameters and a good structure to use as you begin to draft the scene. Look at the next example to see how I built a basic scene by using The Writing Compass.

Character Template Example I

FWM: Mentor Text

> *"The girl appeared to be somewhere in the neighborhood of ten years old.*
>
> *Her small, round face was set with dark eyes, deceptively sweet in appearance.*
>
> *Her hair should have been a sandy yellow color, but its present unwashed state made it appear darker. Her bare feet dangled, grimy with dirt and hued to the color of strong coffee.*
>
> *She sat perched on the low wall that bordered the street and watched the crowd as an owl watches a night field, moving only once to tug the shawl from where it had fallen from one thin shoulder.*
>
> *She was hungrier than she had ever been. Roland had taken her entire haul from the day before—meager as it was— and spent it on liquor. When that was gone, he'd slapped the bowl of thin broth from the table and sent her to bed. The pain in her stomach was driving her now. She would eat, and eat well, before she went home. And Roland could steal his own take.*
>
> *A family of four caught her attention as they passed, grandparents out for a Sunday in the park with a young boy and girl. Gold flashed at the man's waistcoat and on the woman's fingers.*
>
> *She blinked only once, took in the landscape and prepared the strike.*
>
> *Fisting her skirt in her hand, she tipped off the wall and swooped into the crowd, her hungry black eyes never leaving the mark."*
>
> *The Fiction Writing Maps: A Step-By-Step Guide To Characters*

Decoding The Mentor Text

1. The first sentence gives age in a straightforward manner. Since a new character is introduced here, one of the first things the reader wants to know is age and gender. Stick to easy, common methods of conveying that information.

2. As humans, the face is often the first thing we go to. We see eyes right away as they help us determine the mood and mindset of people before we even speak to them. If eyes are a striking color or shape, let it be noted.

3. This third sentence ties into who the character is within the story. She is young and obviously unkempt.

4. This sentence anchors the character in the setting.

5. Her clothes are threadbare and old. Now we know something more about the girl and her place in the social hierarchy.

6. Notice that the outer appearance of the character also conveys an impression of her vulnerability.

7. When possible, give a character something to hold or an activity to engage in.

8. This is information about the ancillary characters in the passage. This sets up the completion of the short scene.

9. Now we see that we probably don't have anything to fear for this urchin. She's astute enough to pick out a watch in a crowd and chase after an easy mark.

Choosing Relevant Details

I used only a few details to begin building this character.

- Blue-eyed
- Dirty
- Old clothes

- Urchin
- Pickpocket
- Ten years old

Applying The Template

1. The character age and outward physical appearance from far away.

2. Moving in closer, notice what is uncommon in your character's face.

3. As you take another step forward, you should be close enough to the character to see strangeness, inconsistencies, smells and physical signs that tell you something more about the character. Everything from how a person's breath smells to the mole beside their mouth can be noticed at this distance.

4. Place the character in the physical space of the setting. Think about describing the specific boundaries as if you were placing the character on a stage. What is she standing on, what's above her, who's beside her, what does she feel if she stretches out her hand and why is that setting important?

5. Once you place the character, give the reader a visual image (or colloquialism) to set the time, place, era, social stratification, etc. for this character before moving on to plot.

6. If possible, give a relevant detail regarding the opening that will set the stage for the story. Remember the rule of threes. Readers need three points of comparison to set a character or event clearly in their mind.

7. What is the character doing or holding and how does that relate to who she is?

8. Next, notice how the character views the setting around her. What is she seeing? This is a good place to have characters notice something descriptive and specific about other characters that might help the reader tag them later in the

9. The last sentence gets your character up and moving to the next plot point. Here, you loop back around to something you noted at the beginning of the scene. Tie the end up in a neat loop before taking off into the next scene. Then go on to the next scene!

> *"How did you and Callie meet?" Charles asked. The two friends were as unlikely a pair as he'd ever seen. Where Callie was bony and boyish, Sio was round and voluptuous. Callie's fiery red waves couldn't be contained by rubber bands, but Sio's sleek blond hair behaved as perfectly as Sio herself. But as certainly as night follows day, you could be sure that a blond head was always right behind the red one.*
>
> *"It was Kindergarten," Sio explained. "That August had been so hot that the air conditioner at school gave out. The teachers sent us all onto the playground. Can you imagine?"*
>
> *Sio had found herself in a crush of children—all of them older, all of them strangers—and one of her shoelaces had come untied. She'd hated school so far—all two hours of it—and she wanted to go home. She'd asked the teacher to call her mother after the first fifteen minutes and been met with a reproachful stare. She wouldn't go find that hatchet-faced woman now and ask for her help.*

So Sio had sat down with her back against a tree and tried to remember how her mother had wound the laces of her pink sneakers into bunny ears.

"I was hot and tired, and ready to cry. Then Calendar appeared.

She was impossibly small and skinny, with a flaming red ponytail on top of her head skewing decidedly to the left. She was like those cans of grapefruit juices and lemonade they sell in the freezer sections. A concentrated version of Calendar before we added water."

Charles gave her a wide-eyed stare. "Good God. That must have been terrifying."

Sio laughed softly. "Wonderfully terrifying."

"Calendar sat down next to me with a look I'll never forget. Imagine those blue eyes in a an even smaller face." She paused for a thoughtful moment before continuing. "she said, 'Watch how I do it. I'm only going to do it once so pay attention as if your life depends on it.'

I'll confess, she scared me a little.

A wry smile played at the corner of Sio's mouth.

"She showed me how to tie the shoe, undid the laces and said, 'It's your turn. You can do this.' And I did it on the first try. I'd never felt so capable, so powerful before. But that isn't what made us friends."

Sio cleared her throat, fighting back the wave of emotion that always came when she remembered that day.

"After I tied my shoe, I asked Calendar if her mother could talk to my mother so she could come over and play." Sio shot a quick glance at Charles and saw the crease cut deeply at the corner of his mouth. This was the one thing they all avoided talking about. The scar their eyes darted over, pretending not to see in order to avoid causing Callie any pain.

"Cal told me that she was an orphan." Sio's voice stumbled over the word. She'd been so careful over the last twenty-three years to avoid the word that she had to force it out of her mouth.

> *"She told me she didn't have a mother who could call my mother. She shrugged it off and said it didn't really matter anyway because she'd figured a way out of school and wouldn't be coming back after lunch. That's when I knew that we were going to be friends."*
>
> *Sio beamed a smile.*
>
> *"Calendar was my ticket home."*

Discussion

As you can see, this Basic Character Introduction of Sio includes a wealth of information that relates to other characters, Calendar primarily. If it wasn't what you expected, that's a point to note. Characters in a novel do not operate independently. They're like threads on a loom that cross again and again. The warp and the weft of characters meeting and leaving, engaging in action and dialogue under varying circumstances gives the fabric of your story its hues and tones. A Basic Character Introduction can provide as much information about other characters as it does about the new character that you're actually introducing.

That said, I could take a small chunk of what I have above and create and even more Basic Introduction for Sio. Something like this:

"Sio and Calendar were an unlikely pair of friends. Where Callie was small and thin, Sio was round and voluptuous. Callie's fiery red waves couldn't be contained by rubber bands, but Sio's sleek blond hair behaved as perfectly as Sio herself. They had met in Kindergarten on the first day of school and run away at recess, sending the town into a panicked search for the missing girls. The two came tumbling out of the forest that bordered the town, having spent the afternoon under the shade of the trees, Sio's blond head bobbing behind Callie's red one. And so it had always been. As certainly as night follows day, one was never far behind the other."

Character Template Example II

1. *Keep this short and precise.*

2. *Describe what's going on at that moment in your story.*

3. *Identify the relationship of the people in the scene.*

4. *Begin to draft your character. Cover the Basic Introduction points presented in Chapter One.*

5. *Make a connection to something that happened in the past. Incorporate some backstory or a vignette that helps to describe who your character is without resorting to a list.*

6. *Let your character open up and divulge something personal. Let him show a fear or a weakness, even if it's only a hint. But keep it relevant. If you're going to mention it here, make certain that it's important enough to mention it later in another iteration.*

7. *Help the reader understand the emotion of the moment. How does your character feel? Readers need to feel their way through a passage in addition to seeing it visually. Tie those feelings into something concrete and make it count.*

8. *One of the elements that makes fiction believable is highlighting the passage of time. The passage of time acts like perspective in a painting, giving the impression of depth and substance, of dimension and volume. Don't be afraid to move back and forth through time, but do it with measured care.*

9. *Divulge something about the character that allows the reader to gauge what kind of person she is. Your character can react to a situation, respond to a memory or dive into action. Show you reader through example what kind of person this would be if they met him on the street.*

10. *Surprise the reader. Readers love surprises. Let your character say something clever, unanticipated or in flagrant violation of his archetype. Hook the reader with novelty.*

11. *End with an idea or emotion that readers can sink their teeth into. Make it the introduction to something you'll touch again and again in the novel with regards to this character.*

"*Since his 14th birthday, things had started to change for Zeke. Not the typical adolescent 'change' like moving to a new city or going to a new school. The change was inward. He'd felt something building for weeks now. Now that energy screamed for him to unleash it. He pointed his finger at the desk where his pencil lay atop his uncompleted homework. Focusing the churning, unsettling storm on the masticated body of the mustard-colored number two pencil, he visualized the tiniest pinprick of an opening through which he willed the energy to move.*"

Clint Wilson. *The Sleeper*

Exploring An Opening Template

If you've ever read prose that was just a little "off," it might have been missing one or more of the key elements I'm about to show you. Nailing all of these elements will virtually ensure that your prose reads at an industry standard level.

When we read, it's easy to become so lost in the story that we lose track of the work the prose is doing. In fact, this is the goal of good writing. A good opening always includes the same elements, much like the Basic Character Introduction. In this section, I'll break them out in numbered sentences and show you the precise work these sentences do.

This prose adheres to a perfect pattern that editors and agents have perfected over the years. Readers have become acclimated to this level of excellence, and anything less feels amateurish.

It isn't as difficult as you might think to hit this standard, but it does require focused attention to very specific details. Let's look at a good example for this and then break the elements down one at a time.

Opening Template

This next piece is from another work by Clint Wilson. I use it as an example of a good opening to a scene with a new character.

> *Absolutely unbelievable. Harold was a law student. He'd taken this philosophy class that his counselor promised would be an easy 'A.' "Introduction to Philosophy— A Humanist Overview" had historically been a course taught by an aging professor, a gnarled old academic named Harrington. Harold's roommate had assured him that Harrington loved the sound of his voice and lectured the entire hour without stopping for questions. The professor hadn't changed his exams or pop quizzes in over a decade and Harold had them saved to his laptop. It was just Harold's luck that this year the old fart had taken off and another professor was called to step in.*
>
> *Apparently, this new guy was the rock star of philosophy professors. The prominent Lionel Cuthbert had the undergrads had clustered around his desk to pay homage. It was as if Sting had shown up at the local music festival. Harold shifted his backpack to the floor and took a seat in the last empty chair. He'd come to class expecting to sleep in the back row.*

The only open seat had been at the far end of the second row—too close to the podium for an overt nap. Damn.

He'd stayed out until after two last night with his roommate for drinks at The Porch, thinking today would be a blow off class. His eyelids already felt heavy and he could feel the frustration of having to keep them open for another hour mounting inside him. He rubbed them hard and glanced to his left. A sweatshirt clad girl sat next to him typing furious notes on her iPad and looking up every few seconds in anticipation of the professor's lecture. What a joke.

Harold reminded himself that he could still change classes without incurring a fee. But the only other course open at this late date was a random English course in feminist literature and the teacher was not a fan of law students—or men. Who knows, he thought, maybe this class would work out even with the new professor. An entire lecture hall wouldn't be so amped with excitement if this professor—what was his name—wasn't excellent in his field. Maybe Harold would even learn something. In the meantime, he tried to nudge himself out of lethargy.

Cuthbert paced behind the podium now, preparing notes and getting his presentation in order. He looked like the poster boy for lifetime academics: his hair was swept back from his forehead in a cut that was too long for any other profession, but perfect for a tousled, diligent professorial look. He sported the Williams & Sons tweeds from four seasons ago, and had just enough of a British accent to hint that he'd studied for at least a few years in the UK.

"Good Morning," Dr. Cuthbert's voice finally rang out across the lecture hall in full, rich tones that reached the very back seat, "today we're going to start with a broad overview of philosophy—from the earliest days of the discipline to our modern era. However, let me begin with some impromptu questions to the class to see where professor Harrington left off last semester and to get an understanding of where our newest arrivals..." here his eyes shifted to Harold's chair.... "are in their understanding of the history of philosophy."

Harold felt his stomach clench at the attention. 'What the hell? How had this guy even known he was new to the class and where his seat was?' With a determination to march straight over to the registrar and switch courses, Harold sat up a little straighter, teeth grinding at the unfairness of it all. He was going to give his counselor a piece of his mind. Shouldn't she know about these changes ahead of time? Wasn't it her job to save high-performing students like himself the agony of situations just like this?

"Open your books—or eBooks—to page 50." Harold winced. He hadn't even bothered to buy the textbook. He'd already spent nearly $2000 on books and the idea of forking over another $150 for a stodgy old philosophy book was more than he could bear. He glanced again to his left, hoping that sweatshirt girl might be amenable to sharing for at least one class. She was onto him, having already identified him as a law student rather than a philosophy major, and was giving him the stick eye over the rim of her tortoise shell glasses. Harold looked back to the podium and caught Dr. Cuthbert looking pointedly at him. The man cleared his throat. "Well, then... we'll do the best we can?" The statement phrased as a question was meant just for him, Harold knew. Every other philosophy geek in here had their technology or the book at the ready. God, if he had to stay in this class, Harold was going to be screwed. He'd be lucky to make a 'C' after the start he'd gotten—and getting even a mediocre grade would take more work than he wanted to do. A stream of epithets ran through his head as he shifted a legal pad from his backpack and prepared to take notes on a class he hoped never to return to. Absolutely unbelievable.

Template For Two Characters

"Every passing day was driving him closer and closer to his destiny. Had you asked him a year ago, he would have told you he was destined to be Florence's greatest artist. He'd discarded that destiny in a bonfire of the vanities long ago and clung now to the more immediate and soothing substitute of alcohol and oblivion. The man's name was Lorenzo

Ricci. The third son and youngest of the five children born to Barone and Baronessa Ricci. He had only the name of his family now with none of the wealth or title afforded to his two older brother. At twenty-eight, he should have made a name for himself as an artist, having gained three major commissions from great Italian families both in Florence and Rome before the age of twenty-four. Until last summer, he had moved in the circles of the rich and powerful with all of the ease of his elder brothers and none of the constraints that polite society demanded. He'd had liaisons with married women, an opera singer, a brief stint with a well-known American actress and another handful of short-term relationships that he'd ended when the mystery wore off. In short, he'd lived like the artist that he was. Or rather, the artist he had been.

Lorenzo sat on the steps under the loggia and watched as the first group of tourists poured from the Piazza della Signoria towards the Uffizi. It was a good crowd today. Filled with Americans. He smiled to himself and tossed back the last of an espresso. The Americans always tipped well, heathens thought they were when it came to art. He could expect to go home with his pockets full. A ray of winter sunlight broke through the clouds and shot down into the piazza della Uffizi just as a woman cut through the crowd.

Like the main character in a movie, she stepped past the tourists and moved forward with a confidence bourne of familiarity. She knew her way around Florence, but she was no Florentine. She was dressed as a tourist, sporting a wide-brimmed hat, low shoes and carrying a messenger bag slung across her chest. Lorenzo followed her progress as she approached the steps of the museum and began ascending. She passed by him without a glance, shuffling the bag from her shoulder as she did, exposing the pale round curve of breast and leaving the heady scent of fig and honey in her wake.

He stood and turned, his cashmere coat swirling around him, dark hair falling in timeless Florentine fashion at the sides of his face as his gaze followed her up the last step and into the darkened doorway. She would be back, he knew. The museum did not open for another ten minutes. The ticket office would send her outside to wait with the others. By then he would be surrounded with tourists clamoring for a guided recitation of the Uffizi's masterpieces. She would join the tour. The pretty ones always did. He had never had to cajole any woman into purchasing a tour or falling into his bed after the tour. But this one.... his confidence wavered for an instant. She must join the tour, he thought.

She emerged from the door just as he had expected and the sight of her coming out of the shadow and into the sunlight made him catch his breath. Involuntarily, his right hand closed as if around a paintbrush. The movement felt as it had in the beginning—natural, powerful, brimming with possibility. The urge to capture her was instinctive. She was built tall and lean, with hair cascading around her face and over her shoulder in waves the color of Botticelli's Venus. But whereas Venus looked back with a dreamy, languid expression, the woman before him regarded the scene with alert green eyes and a vivacity that infused every movement and expression.

For the past six months, Lorenzo hadn't picked up a paintbrush. He'd given himself over to shuffling tourists around during the day and drinking until he reached the mind-numbed state where he could finally fall asleep. In this way, one day bled into the next and he barely felt the march of time towards his own irrelevance. But as this woman stood framed in the doorway, Lorenzo knew that painting her in even such an innocuous setting would result in a masterpiece. "Lady In Doorway" would become the next Mona Lisa. Centuries from now, historians would ponder the identity of this woman. He had to know her, had to meet her.

She nodded her understanding to a guard who gestured her down the steps. Desperation twisted his gut. His eyes searched her face, begging her to see him. She began descending. She would pass him in another step and the moment would be lost. As she came even with him, she paused and glanced over, changing direction towards him—towards a destiny that awaited them both."

Clint Wilson. *Loggia de Lanzi*

Discussion

This template introduces two characters, but focuses on Lorenzo's perception of the events. Notice that the opening follows the Basic Character Introduction and incorporates the elements in a succinct prose. Next, it dives into brief Exposition and gives just enough detail of Lorenzo's backstory to set up the scene. Now that the stage is set, the writer introduces the second character and creates the "problem" of the scene. Notes the effect that her entrance has on Lorenzo and pay attention to his observations that come through the narrative as he outlines her progress into the museum. Once again, the writer dives into Lorenzo's past and describes his liaisons, but now we see the importance of that description. Everything worthy of telling the reader is worth telling at least three times—or leave it out. The fact that Lorenzo has many sexual conquests suddenly becomes important here because of his feelings regarding this one woman. As the excerpt ends, the writer loops back around to end where he started. However, the events of the passage have moved the plot along, introduced the characters and created a powerful connection (for at least one of the characters). This is the work of the scene in a nutshell.

Conclusion

Here's where you pull out all of the writing that you have so far and build it into a scene. You can switch the order around, but keep it simple to get the feel of how to build a scene in small spaces. Don't agonize over language. You can always go back and edit the language after your scene is solidly written.

Templates, as I said before, are simply patterns to play with in your writing. They aren't governed by hard and fast rules. You can move the pieces around to find what works best for you and your characters.

Many times, writers assume that readers know more than they do. Because you live with your characters, you have a familiarity that readers lack, and it's easy to miss details that you take for granted. Use the template as a way to check off the information that you give the reader to make certain all of the key details are included.

It's your turn now to go in and build out the other characters in your novel. You should find that you write more quickly because you know exactly what you need for a basic introduction and are already focused on the goal. Because you've taken some of the uncertainty out of the process, you might find that your writing has become more fluid as you sketch out other characters.

From here, it becomes a joy - rather than a laborious task - to add details, backstory and vignettes for your characters. I encourage you to work in Scrivener as you move through your character building and scene writing. You can find links for Scrivener at www.fictionwritingmaps.com as well as the free Scrivener Template that accompanies a bundled purchase with *A Step-By-Step Guide To Characters.*

Not only is Scrivener a powerful tool, but we have imported all of the character templates and more from *A Step-By-Step Guide To Characters* into The Fiction Writing Maps Scrivener Template.

As additional books in this series become available, we'll add resources to the Scrivener Template to create a one-stop Fiction Writing Maps within the powerful Scrivener software.

I wish you the very best in your writing endeavor and hope your epic novel makes it onto my bookshelf.

All the best,

Jackie St. James

Filmography

A ROOM WITH A VIEW (US/1992) Screenplay by James V. Hart. Based on the novel by Bram Stoker.

BRAM STOKER'S DRACULA (US/1992) Screenplay by Deborah Moggach. Based on the novel by Jane Austen.

HARRY POTTER (US/2001) Screenplay by Steve Cloves. Based on the novel by J. K. Rowling.

INTERVIEW WITH A VAMPIRE (US/1994) Screenplay by Anne Rice. Based on the novel by Anne Rice.

JANE EYRE (US/2011) Screenplay by Moira Buffini. Based on a story by Charlotte Brontë.

PRIDE AND PREJUDICE (US/2005 Screenplay by Lawrence Kasdan. Based on a story by George Lucas and Phillip Kaufman.

RAIDERS OF THE LOST ARK (US/1981) Screenplay by Lawrence Kasdan. Based on a story by George Lucas and Phillip Kaufman.

ROCKY (US/1976) Written by Sylvester Stallone.

THE EMPIRE STRIKES BACK (US/1980) Screenplay by Leigh Brackett, Lawrence Kasdan. Based on an original story by George Lucas.

THE GREAT GATSBY (US/1974) Screenplay by Francis Ford Coppola. Based on the novel by F. Scott Fitzgerald.

THE HOBBIT: AN UNEXPECTED JOURNEY (US/2012) Screenplay by Fran Walsh, Phillipa Boyens, Peter Jackson & Guillermo del Toro. Based on the novel by J. R. R. Tolkien.

THE HUNGER GAMES (US/2012) Screenplay by Suzanne Collins, Gary Ross & Billy Ray. Based on the novel by Suzanne Collins.

THE CHRONICLES OF NARNIA: THE LION, THE WITCH & THE WARDROBE (US/2005) Screenplay by Ann Peacock, Andrew Adamson, Christopher Markus & Stephen McFeely. Based on the novel by C. S. Lewis.

Resources

Character Archetypes

Typical Male Characters

The Hero: The Hero is a usually the main character in a classic adventure. His journey begins in obscurity and follows an arc from humble beginnings through hardship and on to glory. Characterized by the current social ideal of honor, strength and valor, he beats back the forces of darkness and triumphs over the evil that threatens to destroy the fictional setting.

Oppressor: An authoritarian character, this player despises weakness in himself and others and may act in overt, aggression.

Military Hero: Your typical Navy Seal, action figure.

Despot: Type 'A' character who is controlling in the extreme.

Bandit: One who takes from others with little or no remorse.

Typical Female Characters

The Damsel: In order to frame the hero's skills, this quivering damsel is the proverbial "petticoat tied to the railroad tracks." She might bolster the hero, set a baited trap for him or do both throughout the course of the story.

Goddess: Characterized by all things noble and feminine, this player embodies the traditional traits of female allure, comfort and family.

Black Widow: This female character ensnares the Hero through a darker allure.

The Good Woman: This female iteration of character embodies both femininity and inherent goodness. She may either be a wifely ideal or a member of a religious group, either embracing or eschewing her female side.

Wayward Female: This female character breaks the social and norm boundaries by behaving as an independent actor regardless of her relationship ties.

Male or Female Character

Lovers: The typical Rome and Juliet duo that is bound for tragedy.

Unwilling Hero: This Hero needs more than the usual amount of encouragement to engage in the adventure. Even after leaving the comfort of his home, he must be constantly nudged until he finally engages in the plot.

Philanthropist: One who gives a great deal of his time or fortune away. He may or may not be a noble character. His actions may thwart or help the Hero.

Bureaucrat: A pencil-pushing, stick-to-the-rules character.

Caretaker: A character who either literally or figuratively takes care of people, property or secrets.

Weakling: This player is characterized by cowardice and weakness. Though he may keep it somewhat hidden, his shortcoming will be revealed and have significant implications to the group and the plot.

Hermit: Irritable and isolated, this character is unaccepting of company.

Visionary: A character who wants to be something that he or she isn't.

Explorer: This player is driven to wander. He or she might be running from a past wound or event.

Tattler: Always the first to know and willing to tell, this player is the blabbermouth who may either help or hinder the Hero's efforts

Guardian: Protector of the weak and oppressed.

Messenger: A "Cassandra" character whose message is often dismissed as too far-fetched to be believed.

Hunter: This character is the tracker and predator.

Detective: Adept at picking apart puzzles and making sense of intricacies that would elude others, this character is the typical Sherlock Holmes.

Arbiter: This diplomatic character often diffuses dangerous situations or talks the Hero away from conflict that would lead to defeat.

Leader: Always knows the best thing to do—and people follow. Ex: William Wallace

Magician/Wizard/Superpowers: Has special powers or abilities. Ex: Superman, Harry Potter.

Machiavelli: Character whose actions are outside the social limits of acceptable. He or she justifies those actions in standard Machiavellian form.

Scapegoat: The character who willingly throws himself under the bus for the cause.

Pretender: A character who purports to be something he is not.

The Beast: Generally, this character is considered depraved beyond redemption. However, he might be reclaimed by love, sacrifice or knowledge.

Limelight Chaser: A player who constantly views for attention through words and actions.

Revolutionary: One who fights against the status quo in the battle for what he perceives is the greater good.

Rogue: Looks out for himself and no one else. Ex: Han Solo

Turncoat: This character has an ingrained personal flaw that invariably wreaks havoc on the plot.

Good Samaritan: A character who reaches out to help others in meaningful and often uncommon ways.

Academic: Engrossed in research, learning or higher education, this player's gift is discovery and mental labor.

Hedonist: Captivated by elegance and comfort, this character chases degeneracy and debauchery.

Slave: This character lives in either explicit or implicit servitude to another character or situation.

Sycophant: A flattering character who desires a powerful ally or wants to bask in the reflected glow of another, greater character.

Comedian: This character brings light and comic relief to the story.

Urchin: This player exemplifies the weak and frail character in the typical Oliver Twist scenario as either a male of female character.

Fallguy: A character whose death or exit redresses some past wrong. The sacrifice of this character renders him powerful & lends momentum to the plot.

Exile: This character is one who has been turned away from social groups. He may range from unrecognized genius to unfathomable idiot. He may either aid or thwart the success of the hero.

Idealized Partner: This is the partner of the opposite sex who jives with the her on an intellectual, platonic ground.

Rural Innocent: This iteration of the Hero has him not leaving, but returning home to find that everything he held dear has dissolved. As the interloper with an intimate knowledge of the past, he finds solutions that have eluded the other players.

Heroes in Training: Another iteration of the Hero, this character emerges from a pack of similar characters on a quest to achieve a noble objective.

Guide or Mentor: The Guide serves as a tutor or parental figure, a role model and the social conscience of the collective. He departs as the Hero follows his character arc up and arrives each time as the Deus Ex Machina to present the Hero with a piece of knowledge, an insight or a physical weapon that will be necessary for victory in the final battle.

Gatekeeper: This Character holds the keys to the Hero's entrance into the realm of "brotherhood." He may keep the Hero out for a time, but he eventually relents and ushers the Hero into the main conflict.

Parent-Child Conflict: Any of the previous or latter Archetypes can be enhanced with a Parent-Child relationship. This might be tinged with either conflict or love.

Companions as a Tribe: A strong group of friends who undergo a trial together. They may stay closely knit or fall apart as a result of the conflict. However, their past is grounded in another conflict that propels the story forward.

Trusted Supporters: These minor characters usually arrive on the scene to help through a tricky issue. They hold clues to expository information that reveal the Hero.

Villain: The Hero's opponent. The villain often represents the darker side; his job is to provide objective clarity on the murky—and often evil—social and cultural issues that plague the Hero and act as the hub of the plot.

Villain With A Conscience: A villain in opposition to the Hero who is saved by the Hero's compassion and nobility.

Writer's Resources

Livescribe: Livescribe 3 Smartpen Black Edition

Livescribe 2GB Echo Smartpen

Livescribe Extra Notebooks

Scrivener

Scribd

Dragon Naturally Speaking Home 13.0

Suggested Reading

Louise Penny: *The Cruelest Month*

Ramaswamy, Shobha. "*Archetypes in fantasy fiction a study of JRR Tolkien and JK Rowling*" (2010).

http://ir.inflibnet.ac.in:8080/jspui/bitstream/10603/102458/15/15_summing%20up.pdf

Livingston, Michael. "The myths of the author: Tolkien and the medieval origins of the word hobbit." *Mythlore: A Journal of JRR Tolkien, CS Lewis, Charles Williams, and Mythopoeic Literature* 30.3 (2012): 9.

https://dc.swosu.edu/cgi/viewcontent.cgi?referer=https://scholar.google.com/scholar?start=100&q=c.+s.+lewis+tolkien+mentor+&hl=en&as_sdt=0,44&httpsredir=1&article=1130&context=mythlore

Seddon, Eric. "*Letters to Malcolm and the trouble with Narnia: CS Lewis, JRR Tolkien, and their 1949 crisis.*" *Mythlore: A Journal of JRR Tolkien, CS Lewis, Charles Williams, and Mythopoeic Literature* 26.1 (2007): 5.

Letters to Malcolm and the Trouble with Narnia: C.S. Lewis, J.R.R. Tolkien, and Their 1949 Crisis

Eric Seddon

Independent Scholar

http://etheses.whiterose.ac.uk/3886/1/uk_bl_ethos_564500.pdf

McKee, Robert. "Story: Substance." Structure, Style, and the Principles of Screenwriting, Methuen (1999).

Ballenger, Bruce and Barry Lane. Discovering the Writer Within: 40 Days to More Imaginative Writing. Writer's Digest Books, 1989.

Bickham, Jack. The 38 Most Common Fiction Writing Mistakes. Writer's Digest Books, 1997.

Bickham, Jack. Scene and Structure. Writer's Digest Books, 1999.

Dixon, Debra. Goal, Motivation and Conflict: The Building Blocks of Good Fiction. Gryphon Books for Writers, 1999.

Dunne, Peter. Emotional Structure: Creating the Story Beneath the Plot: A Guide for Screenwriters. Linden Publishing, 2006.

Field, Syd. Screenplay: The Foundations of Screenwriting. Dell Publishing Company, Inc. 1984.

Frey, James. How to Write a Damn Good Novel: A Step-by-Step No Nonsense Guide to Dramatic Storytelling. St. Martin's Press, 1987.

Gardner, John. The Art of Fiction: Notes of Craft for Young Writers. Vintage, 1991.

King, Stephen. Secret Windows: Essays and Fiction on the Craft of Writing. Book of the Month Club, 2000.

McKee, Robert. Story: Substance, Structure, Style and the Principles of Screenwriting. Regan Books, 1997.

Provost, Gary. *100 Ways to Improve Your Writing*. Signet, 1985.

Rodale, J.I. The Synonym Finder. Warner Books, 1986.

Swain, Dwight. *Techniques of the Selling Writer*. University of Oklahoma Press, 1982. Vogler, Christopher. The Writer's Journey: *Mythic Structure for Writers*. Michael Wiese

INDEX

A Room With A View, *161*

action, 14, 35, 36, 39, 42, 45, 48, 56, 65, 67, 74, 79, 85, 95, 96, 111, 113, 119, 121, 133, 140, 141, 142, 143, 150, 151, 163

actions, 81, 84, 100, 113, 122, 127, 135, 165, 166, 167

Activating the Character, 57

anecdote, 41, 55, 81, 82, 83, 84, 86, 92, 93

Anecdote, 82, 84

anecdotes, 81, 85, 99

Anecdotes, 81

arc, 74, 92, 163

archetypes, 68, 69, 70, 71, 73, 76, 113

Archetypes, 68, 69, 71, 72, 169, 171

art of creating character, 38

Arthur Conan Doyle, 28, 30, 33, 46, 47, 50, 100, 130, 131, 136

aspects of a character, 32

backstory, 72, 79, 80, 91, 99, 114, 151, 159

Backstory, 77, 79, 135

backstory,, 79, 80

backwards design, 27

body type, 23, 26, 27, 28, 29, 30, 32, 40, 49, 50

C. S. Lewis, 25, *162*

character arc, 85, 93, 129, 168

Character Archetypes, 75, 163

character backstories, 77

character details, 12

character development, 13, 16

character emotion, 41

character introduction, 24, 25, 26, 30, 37, 38, 45, 112

character introductions, 24, 25, 49

character motivation, 11, 57, 58

character motivations, 78

character opening, 39, 140

character traits, 34, 35, 120, 123

character's emotional state, 38

characterization, 32, 40, 42, 50, 53, 56, 114, 159

Characterization, *107*

classic fiction, 13

Classic Fiction, *21, 28, 30, 33, 35, 47, 50, 59, 60, 64, 82, 87, 99, 112, 120, 121, 128, 130, 131, 133, 136*

conflict, 38, 62, 70, 113, 133, 166, 169

conflicts, 78

creative mind, 96, 97

description, 23, 24, 28, 29, 32, 33, 34, 36, 37, 47, 48, 52, 56, 100, 114, 119

dialogue, 34, 36, 37, 84, 119, 140, 141, 142, 143, 150

DRACULA, *161*

Dune, 77

dynamic characters, 15

E. M. Forster, 35, 88, 111, 112

Elizabeth Von Arnim, 33, 120, 121

emotion, 41, 42, 46, 54, 63, 99, 100, 109, 148, 151, 152

Emotion, 37, 46

emotional response, 37

emotions, 37, 52, 99, 100, 105, 135

expectations, 71, 79, 81

exposition, 41, 55, 143

facial features, 23, 32, 34, 41, 55

flaw, 139

FWM, 17, 29, 31, 34, 36, 48, 51, 53, 61, 88, 89, 101, 144

Game of Thrones, 58, 109

Gender and age range, 30

Gone With the Wind, 27

Harry Potter, 38, 108

HARRY POTTER, *161*

height, 23, 26, 28, 30, 126

hero, 28, 70, 72, 73, 74, 94, 125, 128, 129, 131, 134, 135, 136, 164, 168

Hero, 69, 71, 72, 128, 163, 164, 165, 166, 168, 169

Heroic Traits, 125, 137

history, 21, 77, 78, 79, 80, 81, 84

inner life of the character, 38, 48

INTERVIEW WITH A VAMPIRE, *161*

J. K. Rowling, 38

JANE EYRE, *161*

JK Rowling, *171*

JRR Tolkien, *171*

Lady Caroline, 120, 121, 122

Livescribe, *105, 170*

Lord of the Rings, 127

Louise Penny, *86, 171*

Mark Twain, 96, 98

mood, 42, 121, 145

motivation, 64, 65, 66, 85, 95, 99

Narnia, *171*

narrative, 12, 30, 34, 76, 79, 84, 96, 97, 114, 141, 142, 143

Narrative, 140

novel design, 9

novel writing, 13, 14, 16

observation, 140

observations, 46, 84, 111, 141

opening scene, 41

Parsing History, 92

physical appeal, 32, 55

physical reaction, 54

physical traits, 26, 52

Physical Traits, 52

plot, 9, 10, 13, 26, 28, 31, 34, 43, 47, 48, 49, 51, 52, 56, 66, 68, 69, 70, 72, 80, 81, 82, 86, 92, 101, 106, 111, 113, 119, 124, 138, 142, 146, 147, 165, 167, 168, 169

plot point, 34, 52, 124, 138

point of view, 41, 92

Pride and Prejudice, 25, 82, 136

PRIDE AND PREJUDICE, *161*

Project Gutenberg, 17

quick character sketches, 51

quick path to character, 27
Quick Write, 114, 115
RAIDERS OF THE LOST ARK, *161*
reader rapport, 45
resources, 11
response, 140
responses, 46, 54, 113, 122, 140, 141
Rocky, 73, 74
ROCKY, *161*
Scaffolding, 52, 70
scaffolding techniques, 30
Scarlett O'Hara, 27, 125
scene, 140
Scene, 10, 11, 143
Scrivener, *13, 109, 110, 159, 170*
setting, 28, 37, 49, 54, 110, 111, 145, 163
Setting, 10, 11, 140
Sherlock Holmes, 46, 49, 99, 129, 135, 166
simple narratives, 27
Sir Arthur Conan Doyle, 25, 27, 51
story, iv, 9, 16, 17, 23, 24, 25, 27, 34, 35, 38, 42, 45, 52, 56, 57, 62, 68, 69, 70, 73, 74, 75, 76, 81, 82, 92, 93, 94, 97, 106, 107, 109, 110, 111, 117, 118, 122, 125, 126, 129, 134, 140, 145, 150, 151, 164, 168, 169
story premise, 38
storytelling, 84
strong character, 33, 107
symbol, 36, 107, 108, 109, 110, 111, 112, 113, 114, 117, 119, 120, 121, 122, 124
symbolism, 114, 119, 122
Symbolism, 107, 111, 123
Symbols, 107, 108, 109, 114, 117, 119, 122
Template, 110, 143, 144, 146, 151, 152, 159
The Adventures of Sherlock Holmes, 25, 28, 30, 33, 46, 47, 50, 100, 130, 131, 136
The Adventures of Tom Sawyer, 96, 97, 98
THE CHRONICLES OF NARNIA, *162*
THE EMPIRE STRIKES BACK, *161*
THE GREAT GATSBY, *161*
THE HOBBIT, *162*
The Hunger Games, 43, 62, 64, 129
THE HUNGER GAMES, *162*
THE LION, THE WITCH & THE WARDROBE, *162*
The Short List, 24
The Sorcerer's Stone, 38
thoughts, 19, 40, 41, 54, 55, 56, 66, 67, 75, 76, 81, 84, 86, 92, 93, 105, 122, 123, 124, 127, 128, 130, 135, 137, 138, 139, 140, 141
Tolkien, 20, 78, 81, 114, 162, 171
traits, 34, 68, 70, 73, 76, 92, 93, 119, 120, 121, 122, 123, 125, 126, 127, 131, 134, 164
transition, 38
trustworthiness, 32, 55
Vignette, *88, 94, 99, 101, 105, 106*
vignettes, 76, 99, 106
villain, 70, 71, 72, 73, 74, 94, 127, 134, 169
Villain, 72, 169
visual cues, 46

willpower, 138
Willpower, 126, 132
writing characters, 15, 94

Writing in a Loop, 87
writing process, 10, 16